WITHDRAWN

WITHDRAWN

Missionary Kid (MK)

by
Edward E. Danielson, Ph.D.

Faith Academy
Manila, Philippines

LIBRARY
BRYAN COLLEGE
DAYTON, TENN. 37321

74474

Scripture quotations are from the New American Standard
Bible, copyrighted by the Lockman Foundation, 1960. 1962, 1963,
1968. 1971, 1973, 1975. and are used bv permission

Acknowledgements: The author wishes to express his
appreciation to Lucille Nickel for her valuable and extensive
help in typing and editing, and to the photography students
at Faith Academy for the photos.

Copyright, 1982, by Edward E. Danielson. All rights
reserved. Printed in Manila, Philippines. No part of this
book may be used or reproduced in any manner whatsoever.
without permission of the publisher, except in the case of
brief quotations in articles and reviews.

For information, write Edward E. Danielson. Ph.D. at:

Faith Academy   or   c/o Mission Aviation Fellowship
Box 820   Box 202
Makati. Rizal   Redlands, CA 92373
PHILIPPINES

To

John and Debbie,

two outstanding MKs

and

to Louise, the one

most responsible for

their nurture in Christ.

INDEX

FOREWORD

It is with pleasure that I endorse this valuable work of Dr. Danielson.

For some years now I have felt there was a need for Christians to
be better informed on the subject of educating missionaries' children.
Each additional bit of information should help Christians to know how to
pray more efficiently and for missionary administrators and parents as
they seek to develop better means of meeting the needs of the missionary
child.

If the unreached people of our world are to be reached with the gospel, families will need to continue to answer God's call. When this
happens, education of the children in the family is crucial.

Dr. Danielson draws on his educational background and experiences
as well as findings from his research in presenting this book. He has
held almost every possible position in schools for missionaries' children, including maintenance, superintendent, boarding home parent. teacher,
guidance counselor, and is currently a school psychologist.

Ed and his wife, Louise, who has been a faithful secretary at Faith
Academy. seem to have an exceptional understanding of the make up and
needs of missionary children. Besides their different positions in
schools for missionaries' children, they were able to guide their own
son. John, and daughter, Debbie. through various educational experiences
on the mission field. including an international day school and one year
as boarding students in Honduras while Ed directed the youth work of
national churches in Costa Rica. Both John and Debbie graduated from

Faith Academy.

I would like to encourage mission leaders as well as missionaries and their friends to read and share the contents of this book with those of like interest.

Donald D. Boesel. Superintendent
Faith Academy
Manila. 1982

PREFACE

Take this as fair warning. The author of this book is biased. He favors MKs (missionaries' kids) and looks upon them as perhaps the most valuable human resource today. He may stand up to those who generalize that MKs are people with serious emotional and adjustment problems, or that they have been neglected and abandoned.

But since he is aware of his strong affections for MKs, he has taken pains to research the personality development of MKs in accordance with scientific methods, using statistical analysis.

The numerous personal observations and experiences are based on more than twenty-five years of missionary service with a concentration in the field of education for missionaries' children.

An emphasis on the boarding school student may be noticed. The thrust in that direction is due to the fact that the majority of missionaries have chosen boarding schools as the best option for their children at least for some years of elementary or secondary education.

We believe that this book should be a part of every missionary orientation program and of every class on missions. It is a handbook with practical suggestions for missionary candidates and parents. Some missionaries will find it helpful to give copies to those friends and relatives who have some reservations about children living overseas.

INTRODUCTION

MK is the abbreviation for missionaries' kids. Like many nicknames, the origin cannot be traced, although it seems logical that it is related to PK, the common title for preachers' kids.

We make no apology for using the term even to those who may have grown up with the expression, "If I'm a kid you're a goat. You stink, and I don't." We make no apology because we did not invent nor choose the title. If it had been our choice we might have decided on MC for missionaries' children.

In writings over the years the use of MK has become more and more common, in spite of the fact that other titles have been used in some articles. "Mish-kid" was used in one article, but we've not seen it since nor heard it used in conversation. The term "third culture kids" (TCK) has also been printed in numerous studies, articles and books, but it includes other children living overseas, such as dependents of embassy employees, businessmen and military personnel.

Nor can we refer to them in the manner that one author has as "normal." He writes on this subject that his dealings with these students "confirms a growing distaste for the solecism terming them as MKs and their schools as MKs' schools." (Lockerbie, 1975, P. 27)

At any rate, MKs are not normal. They are well above average and we have the data of scientific research to support this.

When I first read the statement quoted above, my intuitive self said, "This doesn't seem true." But rather than make "guesstimates"

7

we surveyed a random sampling of 104 MKs from the Philippines, Indonesia and Spain, with the following question: "How do you feel about being classified as an MK?" The majority (79%) responded positively, frequently using strong terms such as privileged, proud, special, great, superior, important and cool. Samples of responses are listed below:

"I've been an MK all my life and it's fine with me. It makes me feel like I'm really someone. It seems like with the name comes lots of benefits that normal kids wouldn't have."

"I love it, I think we have more opportunities than those in the U.S."

"I don't mind being called an MK because it puts you in a different class than a lot of other people. You can usually have many experiences that other kids could not have."

"It's true, so there is nothing wrong with it."

"I think it's an honor."

"I don't really mind being called an MK. Actually it's fun being one. You get to move all the time. At least that's what has happened to me. You get to make new friends all the time."

"I don't mind it. I love it."

"I think it is great! It means that I am the child of two people who are following God's will. I think it sort of makes me special, special in a couple of ways. I have

8

listed one already, and another is that they even recognize me to be one."

"I guess I haven't really thought about it before. I guess I feel kind of glad. I'm glad to have the opportunity to be one."

"I don't mind being called an MK, because that's what I am. Anyone that has misconceptions about how MKs are supposed to be like just hasn't met enough."

"It really doesn't matter but if the person knows that we are an MK then we should try harder to impress upon them how 'good' we are."

"I am proud to be an MK."

"I would feel flattered. I consider MKs special and extra good. Only problem, I'm not an MK."

In all fairness, we didn't tabulate the last comment.

There does seem to be a difference of reaction to certain types of people in the home country who tend to stereotype or pigeonhole missionaries' children as "goody-goodies." Actually these individuals don't ordinarily use the term MK because they are not familiar with it. Sixteen percent of the answers indicated this reaction, as suggested in the following responses:

"Well, sometimes I feel special (most of the time). Only when people have the wrong idea about MKs do I not like it; like when

9

they think MKs are perfect, etc. But otherwise I enjoy being called one."

"I don't mind at all being called an MK because I think that we have many more opportunities than regular kids have. I know people in the States who have lived in the same house all their lives, they don't get to see the world like we do. Once in a while people tease you for being an MK but not often, and all it does is make you a little embarrassed."

"It is pretty neat and I am thankful for being an MK. I have so many opportunities to meet people, see places and learn things. Sometimes in the States it gets me down though because I feel like a museum specimen and people look up to me or watch me too much. Also I get stuck with crummy clothes and have to live a different kind of life from my friends."

A very small percentage, 5%, expressed themselves with strong "distaste" as the following student did:

"I think it stinks because when people call you an MK they think of some poor slob that just came out of the bushes in Africa, but most of us are just as well off as they are or even better."

While we were in the process of the survey, one girl after responding asked me why we were asking such a question. When I read the statement quoted earlier she responded emphatically with a look of disbelief on her face, "He should ask an MK!"

To resist a classification to which we obviously belong is to resist reality and may give a glimpse of one's own self esteem.

We use the term MK with no reservations. Other forms, such as missionaries' children, are used only for variation and variety.

GOD'S INTEREST IN MISSIONARIES' CHILDREN

Boony Stomping

Looking closely at a World War II mortar in our son's room I noticed how clean it was. It was caked with corrosion the last time I had seen it. The mortar was one of many World War II relics which the boys at Faith Academy had collected from the caves and fields surrounding the school. "Boony stomping," they called it, from the Tagalog word, bundok, meaning mountain. It had often reminded me of when I was a boy growing up in Michigan and Colorado and had searched for Indian arrowheads.

Faith Academy is an MK (missionary kid) school twelve miles outside of Manila in the Philippines. The Japanese soldiers retreated to the area and entrenched there as their last stand against MacArthur's return to liberate Manila.

I looked at the mortar again. Like much of the old ammunition found in the area, it had not been exploded. Every now and then we would read or hear of Filipinos who had been killed or injured by grenades they had uncovered.

How had he managed to get the mortar so clean, I mused. No doubt he had used some type of solvent. So I asked him, "How did you get it so clean?" His response was, "With a hammer and screw driver."

My heart went either to my head or my intestines, I'm not certain which.

For years I had wondered about the theology of guardian angels.

Perhaps it cannot be substantiated by scripture but this and other experiences were strong indication that if there are such angels, they must be very active in the midst of some MKs.

A Volatile Situation

That same year some of the Senior boys in the dorm which we supervised put together some home made bombs, without fully realizing what they had done. It was Halloween and I had openly bragged on our boys who hadn't gotten into trouble that evening. I knew they were capable of trouble, but was somewhat proud that it was not our boys who had brought down the wrath of a girls' dormparent when they papered the boarding unit. Those boys were in hot water, and were punished perhaps too sternly.

About three weeks later, the boarding superintendent told me that a neighbor had been driving by our dorm on Halloween and saw a fire in their rear view mirror and several American looking boys. They had interpreted it as meaning that our dorm students had put kerosene on the road and lit it after the car had passed. I told the boarding superintendent that I didn't think our boys had done it, but if so I was reasonably certain of which ones might be responsible and would check it out.

For some reason the whole idea struck me as humorous. Perhaps it was because as a teenager I had done a few exciting things at Halloween time. Once there was a dummy which was placed on the road with a rope attached. When a car drove by it was pulled into the bushes before

13

the driver could get out to investigate.

With these humorous thoughts still on my mind I went to the room of the four boys who, I felt, might have been involved. I couldn't keep a straight face. Finally I said, "Look, it's been too long since this happened so there won't be any punishment, but I'd like to know what happened." There were second thoughts about the amnesty which I had granted when they began to explain how they had made some Molotov cocktails, a type of homemade bomb. It was a volatile situation. They had no idea that it was a bomb, but thought it was like a large firecracker. To make it worse, we discovered that what they thought was kerosene was actually gasoline.

What the driver had interpreted as flaming kerosene on the road was actually a home-made bomb flying through the air with a large lighted fuse. It exploded and almost scared the wits out of the boys. They ran to the area where it had exploded to stamp out the weed fire which it had ignited. That's when the driver saw them.

Earlier they had thrown one near the boys who were returning from papering the girls' dorm, but it had not gone off. As soon as they realized what they had, they buried the rest.

Do I believe in guardian angels? Perhaps. Beyond a shadow of a doubt the Lord takes an interest in children who are not able to take care of themselves and perhaps He assigns an extra batallion to MKs.

The Lord Himself, in response to the inquiry as to who is greatest in the Kingdom of God, chose children as His example. (Matt. 18) The great-

est in the Kingdom - children, with all their needs, but with unex-
celled faith.

Train Up a Child

Since we have worked with MKs in boarding schools, people often
ask questions such as, "Do you think it's right to separate children
from their parents?" During one furlough year, while people were asking
questions such as this, we visited fellow graduates of the Bible College
which we had attended. Our children, who had lived in a boarding school
separated from us were doing fine. But the children of several of our
classmates were suffering serious problems. A son was in jail for possession of heroin and faced a prison sentence. Another boy had run
away to marry a girl not approved of by his parents. In four families,
daughters had been divorced. One son had written a book about his reasons for leaving the Christian faith. In all of these and other cases,
we personally know that our classmates had done their utmost to train up
their children in the Lord (Prov. 22:6), while sending them to public
schools. So we asked ourselves which was better, to have the children
at home and go the way of the world, or to have them trained in an MK
boarding school.

For some reason American Christians have the idea that training up
a child in the Lord means that they must be at home.

A pastor whom we admire and love was conducting seminars for
missionaries in the Manila area. As we shared lunch together I asked
him and his wife what they thought of boarding schools. Their response

indicated that children should not be placed in boarding homes because the scriptures tell us to "train up a child" in the way he should go.

"Do you think we at Faith Academy are not training up children in the way they should go?" I asked. "If training them up means in the home then we shouldn't even send them to public schools, but do as they did in Old Testament times with the father teaching in the home."

As the conversation continued I quoted from Matt. 19:29, what is believed to be a prerequisite to missionary service, "and everyone who has left houses or brothers or sisters or father or mother or children... for My name's sake, shall receive as many times as much..."

The pastor stated that he didn't think children were included in the verse to which we responded that the word children does not appear in the parallel passages, but that it does in Matthew.

We discussed the teaching situations found in the Bible. Many of these were boarding situations. Moses, and Samuel are examples. Samuel's case is particularly applicable. Eli, the temple priest, taught Samuel whom his mother had brought to live with him, separated from his parents. Eli's own sons who lived in the same home became wicked (I Sam. 2:12) and the sin of these sons "was very great in the Lord's sight."

One of the keys to Samuel's success is found in his mother Hannah's commitment. She said to her husband, "After the boy is weaned, I will take him and present him before the Lord, and he will live there always." (I Sam. 1:22)

That evening, as the pastor and I were saying our goodbyes, he said, "I guessed you noticed from the way I responded during the question and answer session that I've changed my thinking about MK boarding schools." It was true, he had modified his stance. It's always a pleasure to witness what changes the Lord can work in each of us. I only pray that I might be as open to change as was this outstanding pastor.

Not only were boarding school situations common in Old Testament time but they are more recent than many people realize. Apprenticeship often means boarding with a master craftsman. In Central America we noticed years ago that children are often sent off to larger cities to live with friends or relatives while attending school. This practice is especially true on the secondary level in many parts of the world. It has not been many years in the U.S. since children frequently did the same. Schools have not always been within a few minutes drive from most homes.

Prep schools are receiving a lot of fire today. An actual review of the history of these schools indicate that the majority of our nation's great leaders attended such institutions.

The parents of the boy in jail for possession of heroin mentioned earlier shared with us that their daughter seemed to be going in the same direction as her brother. For us this was extremely disheartening since we knew that they were such dedicated Christian parents, and outstandingly used in children's work. But as they continued their account of how their daughter was growing in the Lord, we became excited with them. Their solution had been the very one most American Christians would avoid. They had sent her to a Christian boarding school in another state. The

17

daughter's attitude had changed, she demonstrated a love for the school as well as for the Lord.

God loves these children, each one, and He is able to meet their needs, even in boarding schools. A third generation missionary was given a verse by his father, a verse which seems to fit here (Rosenau, 1973, p. 57):

"The children of thy servants will continue, and their descendants will be established." (Psalm 102:28)

CHRISTIAN COMMITMENT

Wouldn't it be wonderful if every missionary leaving for foreign soil really had given all to Christ? The assumption is that they have done that. Yet in almost every country we find some reservations about commitment. There are wives who will not allow their husbands to travel or to stay away from home overnight even for an evangelistic or church-related activity. There are others who emphatically say they will never send their children off to school!

A Presentation to Christ

Just before writing this my wife, Louise, and I were going over the Lord's many blessings to us. We are both in reasonably good health. Our children are living for the Lord. We agree that the Lord has blessed us with many rich experiences. Personally, I feel that the Lord could not have blessed me with a better spouse. When we first went to the mission field it was not because one talked the other into it. We had both given our bodies to the Lord in keeping with Romans 12:1,2. Salvation is the free gift that we received, commitment to serve Him was a further step of faith. One year we lived in a remote village of Honduras. The wife of the couple who replaced us was so concerned about their welfare that she would not allow the husband to travel. All the time we were there I never once heard Louise complain of my traveling about and preaching for days at a time. She believed that since we had dedicated ourselves to Christ that it was up to Him to take care of us.

But there were lessons to learn. At times I felt that I should still have control of the future. There were three things I said I would never do. The first was to work in Mexico, the second to join a certain mission, and the third was to drive down the Pan American highway to language school in Costa Rica. As you might have guessed, we ended up doing all three. The Lord did not make us go against our will, He just made us willing to go.

It has been suggested by some Christian counselors that lack of giving all to Christ sometimes results in the serious psychological problems which are attributed to "middle age crisis." (Solomon, 1971) Since such problems seem to be on the increase on the mission field today, it may cause one to question the extent of current commitment and dedication of missionaries.

Presenting one's body to Christ includes its location, as well as consumption and output. Christians cannot advance beyond a certain point in their own walk with the Lord without doing this. I wonder how many people have shared with me that they knew they were Christians, but that they didn't want to present themselves to God for fear He'd make them do something that they didn't want to or make them give up something they didn't want to. Yet in the majority of these cases when they gave in to the Lord He made it very clear that they were to stay where they were and do what they were doing.

The pattern is the same with missionaries. Often, once parents have truly committed their child to Christ they discover he may be kept at home. Almost 50% of the student body at the largest MK school in the world sleep

20

at home, rather than in a dormitory. The whole process is very much like Abraham's sacrifice of Isaac. What he offered to God he was able to keep and enjoy.

Commitment to the cause of Christ seems to involve sacrifice and dedication. This is particularly true when it comes to children in the family.

Separation from Possessions, Friends and Relatives

Like most missionaries we have heard the many reasons which people give for not taking a personal part in the great commission to preach the Gospel to all the world. These reasons, or perhaps excuses, seem to involve an unwillingness to part with personal possessions and to be separated from relatives, including parents, brothers and sisters. Even more difficult is the decision to leave the immediate family for the sake of Christ.

The Lord, Himself, provided the promise that He would give dividends of one hundredfold as well as everlasting life to those who would forsake houses and farms (possessions), brothers, sisters, parents or children. "And everyone that hath forsaken houses or brethren, or sisters or father or mother or wife or children or lands for my name's sake, shall receive a hundredfold, and shall inherit everlasting life." (Matthew 19:29) The word "left" also has the meaning of to lay aside, let alone, send away or yield up. Let every missionary, yea every Christian, ask himself if he is willing to lay aside, leave, let alone, send away or yield up, houses or brothers or sisters or father or mother or children or land.

Total commitment may be illustrated by reference to ham and eggs. For the chicken it's a donation, for the pig it's total commitment.

We have noticed two extremes among missionaries in their commitment to Christ regarding their children. On the one hand there seems to be total abandonment and on the other a commitment with reservations.

Total Abandonment of Children

While visiting an MK school my wife and I were asked to deliver a message to a fellow missionary. His daughter had been in and out of the hospital several times and doctors felt that part of her problem was emotional. They were requesting the parents to visit her. We were glad to oblige especially as the student was such a sweet little thing.

Several days later we arrived at the missionary guest house where the girl's parents worked. We located the father working on the construction of a new guest house. He continued his work as we passed the time of day. Finally I got to the point and notified him that his daughter was in the hospital. In disgust he said to me, "What! She's sick again? She's always sick!" He continued working. Then I told him that the doctors felt that they should go and visit her. Still he continued working. Then he emphatically informed us that he couldn't go but perhaps the mother could. He didn't lose a moment of time in work while we conversed. But I suspect that he lost something else, perhaps a daughter.

Today there stands a sturdy, well constructed, missionary guest home which that father built. He didn't receive a very high salary for his efforts and he worked overtime day after day. Since that day there has been a strange twist of events. Rebels have taken over most of the country and it looks like soon there will be no missionaries there to enjoy a meal or a night's sleep in that structure. Maybe even now it is in the hands of rebels.

Perhaps in the builder's mind he sacrificed more than should be expected. From another viewpoint it looks like abandonment, not sacrifice. I will never forget the frustration and hopelessness we felt in that situation.

Fortunately only a small percentage of missionaries seem to look on boarding schools as a place to get rid of their children while they go about God's work. It's difficult for a child to understand a loving God who would require their parents to be so busy for Him that they have no time for their children.

We have actually known of parents to be in the town of their children's boarding school and not take time to visit them. This has taken place on more than one occasion. Our only consolation is that those who seem to abandon their children are perhaps less than 1% of the missionary population.

Reserved Commitment

The reserved commitment in serving Christ, becomes apparent when parents leave, write or visit their children. They tend to emphasize and re-emphasize how lonely it is without their children. Soon the children get the idea that they should be lonely too, and that's what happens.

When they visit their children, they can't seem to enjoy regular games and activities like they do at home. They spend their time in serious conversations rather than playing catch or swimming. They bring junk food or home baked goods, as though to say "They don't feed you well there." They give lengthy and detailed instructions on how to conduct oneself, as though the staff is not doing this.

Sometimes this is done in the name of honesty and openness. We believe in both but we also see the Lord's priority on thinking about "whatever is true, whatever is honourable, whatever is right, whatever is pure, whatever is lovely, whatever is of good repute, if there is any excellence and if anything worthy of praise, let your mind dwell on these things." (Phil. 4:8) To admit that all things are not perfect is fine, but we must keep returning to the positive. If we keep expressing our feelings to children we may find that they end up with the same feelings. The real problem is in us. The lack of total commitment is in our lap.

Reserved commitment results in overprotection of the type which is described above. Years ago a national pastor shared with us an example of an extreme case of overprotection. The missionary parents of a small child carried with them a bottle of alcohol and some cotton. Whenever their child touched something they would rub his hands with alcohol. MKs laugh at this account, for they well know how impossible it would be to live under such circumstances. That couple, incidentally, did not last long on the mission field.

Another missionary wife explained how she made certain that the house girl did not touch her child while she was away from home. After putting the child to bed, the mother would attach small threads to the door which

24

would be broken if anyone opened the door. She advocated that all missionaries do the same. Personally, we never employed the idea. It seemed wiser to not leave our children than to leave them with someone we felt would harm them. Actually, we had several helpers over the years in whom we had complete confidence.

These extreme forms of overprotection, caused by certain reservations which parents have, seem to be interpreted by children as rejection or disapproval. Since Mother and Dad do everything for them, they come to believe that they are incapable of doing anything on their own. In adulthood these MKs may continue a life of overdependence, and may choose a life partner on the basis of how much that spouse is willing to do for them. They may look upon any relationship as a means of receiving rather than giving.

Dedication of Children

Dedication seems best illustrated in Scriptures by Hannah when she prayed:

> "...O Lord of hosts, if Thou wilt indeed look on the affliction of Thy maidservant and remember me and not forget Thy maidservant, but wilt give Thy maidservant a son, then I will give him to the Lord all the days of his life, and a razor shall never come on his head." (I Samuel 1:11)

Something stirs within my own heart when I recall how Louise and I stood beside the crib of our own children and dedicated them to the Lord. We had no idea what the future might hold for them but we knew He did. We

could pray with Hannah:

"My heart exults in the Lord, My horn is exalted in the Lord,

My mouth speaks boldly against my enemies. Because I rejoice

in Thy salvation. There is no one holy like the Lord. Indeed

there is no one like Thee, nor is there any rock like our God."

(I Sam. 2:1,2)

It would seem well to season the above with three other verses. First, to

emphasize the parents' responsibility to provide for their children:

"But if anyone does not provide for his own, and especially

for those of his household, he has denied the faith and is

worse than an unbeliever." (I Timothy 5:8)

Secondly, missionaries should emphasize the positive:

"Finally, brethren, whatever is true, whatever is honorable,

whatever is right, whatever is pure, whatever is lovely,

whatever is of good repute, if there is any excellence and

if anything worthy of praise, let your mind dwell on these

things." (Phil. 4:8)

And lastly, we must trust Him to meet all of our needs and those of our

children:

"And my God shall supply all your needs according to His

riches in glory in Christ Jesus." (Phil. 4:19)

Summary

The point of this chapter has been to challenge Christians, and especially missionaries, to present their bodies to Christ, and dedicate all possessions, friends and relatives to Him. Some prospective missionaries and some actually on the field, have plainly said, "God you may have everything but my children." In some cases believers do this even before there are any children. How much better it would be to intrust all to the Lord, for He will meet all our needs and those of our children.

HISTORY OF MK SCHOOLS

We are still awaiting the arrival on the scene of an industrious, dedicated individual who will research and document a history of MK schools. It will doubtlessly be a tedious task since the source of records may be letters which missionaries wrote to friends and relatives regarding their children.

Missionaries have learned that supporters back home want information, primarily, about the nationals or "natives" with whom they work. Interest is heightened and offerings given in proportion to the darkness of the nationals' skin and their need for clothing. Therefore, the missionary on deputation hesitates to talk about the subject closest to his own heart, his children.

William Carey is considered by many to be the father of modern missions, which places that era as starting in the 1790's. From that time to near the end of the next century, missionaries' children were generally returned to the country of their citizenship for schooling.

David Livingston was separated from his family for a period of sixteen years on one occasion. He has been quoted as stating the following in a lecture at the University of Cambridge:

"You can hardly tell how pleasant it is to see the blooming cheeks of young ladies before me, after an absence of sixteen years from such delightful objects of contemplation." (Neill, 1965, p. 315)

Adoniram Judson, missionary to Burma, buried one wife and several children on the field.

J. Hudson Taylor, founder of the China Inland Mission (now Overseas Missionary Fellowship), had a vision not only for the Chinese but for the children of missionaries. He felt that these children should be educated on the field. In response to this vision, a school was opened in Chefoo, China in 1881. The Chefoo school was the forerunner of all other MK schools.

When the Communists took over the country in 1949 soldiers occupied and controlled the school. Over a period of time the children were evacuated. Many stories have been related about the miraculous ways in which the Lord protected these MKs.

Although the original Chefoo school was closed, the name did not die. Other MK schools with the same name came into existence. During the centennial year of the founding of the Chefoo school, a book was published which is recommended reading for those interested in MKs. (Miller, 1981)

Taylor's vision for on-the-field training of missionaries' children cannot be overemphasized. His thinking in this area was as revolutionary as many of his other ideas. Once the Chefoo school was opened, missionaries around the world were assured that such a thing could be done. MKs could remain on the field rather than be returned to the home country for their education.

Some of the MKs who attended those early schools relate stories of traveling sometimes for days over rough trails to get to their school. They traveled in ox carts, on horse and mule, carried by coolies in coaches, or simply walked.

29

Vacations were all but unknown to these early MKs. The school years were shorter than they are today. Seven months was considered sufficient. Academically the students did well, missing or skipping years generally for health reasons rather than for lack of ability. It was not uncommon for these students to be put ahead a grade when returning to the country of their parents' citizenship. Up until World War II very few high school students were educated on the field. Students were returned to their home country as soon as they were ready for secondary education. High schools did appear on the scene in the years following the Second World War. As of 1979 there were approximately nine thousand school age missionaries' children living in foreign countries. High Schools on the field are common enough today that no missionary need be forced to send his children home, although he may find it necessary to send him out of the country in which he works. Missionaries leaving for the regions beyond today may be assured that their children may remain relatively close to their field of service.

As missions have developed, the furlough structure has been modified. A one year furlough was expected for each family every four or five years at the beginning of the century. Originally several months time might have been consumed in travel. Medical attention on the field was nothing special. Therefore a whole year for rest and recuperation was needed. The one year furlough also worked out well for the education of the children. Rather than to have the children change school in mid-year, they were able to complete an entire year during the furlough.

Shorter furloughs present special problems when it comes to the children's education, but most mission boards are willing to make arrangements to provide the best situations for MK schooling. In fact, few other organizations extend or shorten terms of service to facilitate the education of the employees' children like missionary societies do.

Mission organizations have observed over the years that children seem to adjust more readily to the foreign cultures if they are either born on the field, or leave for the field as a pre-schooler. One gets the impression that up through the 1950's the majority of missionaries left for their place of service in their early twenties. Three years of study in a Bible Institute was considered adequate preparation. Since then, an emphasis on higher degrees has increased the average age of departure. The author recalls having read in the mid 1970's that the average age of missionaries leaving for the first time to Latin America was 30 years and to Asia, 29 years. It follows that the children are likewise older when first coming to the field. Developmental psychologists stand basically united regarding the importance of the first five years of life. Although it might be assumed that transferring children to a second culture during those critical first five years would be detrimental, studies to date indicate that it has not been true in the case of MKs. (Danielson, 1981) This speaks well for the way in which missionaries handle the transfer. It also speaks well of the Lord's fulfillment of His promises.

As to the future of missions and its effects on MKs, we believe there will be more mobility. Even now we are experiencing the evacuation of

31

missionaries from various countries. Recently we talked to three families who had to leave with just the few items which they could grab from their homes before fleeing. Even the beds were left made.

Shorter furloughs are also affecting the mobility of MKs and their families. The three to six month furloughs which some missions are advocating may work well for single missionaries or those without children, but are more challenging when it comes to children of school age.

Most MK schools have not been able to switch to the shorter furlough system for staff members because of the difficulty of changing in mid year.

Whatever the future does hold, we may rest assured that the Lord will continue to watch over His own people.

SCHOOLS ESPECIALLY FOR MISSIONARIES' CHILDREN

Hot Houses

My wife and I have always enjoyed plants and gardening. At one MK school which I directed I was accused of making it into a park.

We seldom pass up an opportunity to visit flower or garden shows. On the mission field it has been possible to shower Louise with Orchids, not just the flowers, but the plants.

I will not claim to be all knowledgeable in the area of horticulture, but I do know some basic things, which are general knowledge. The first principle is that plants grow best in a certain type of ecology. In the Philippines we discovered that orchids which will not produce in Manila, do exceptionally well in a small town 15 miles out of the city.

There is, we believe, a parallel between plants and people. Certain settings tend to produce distinctive qualities in people. I believe the Lord might refer to them as "peculiar people." (I Peter 2:9)

No doubt this line of reasoning is pragmatic, but why not? If plants grow best in a green house, let's grow them there. If missionaries' children develop best in schools designed for them, let's place them there.

Every now and then someone refers to MK schools as hot house environments. I never correct people when they approach me with this line of argument. After all they are right. Missionary children are in a hot house, separated from much of the world while they are at school. They are insulated from certain elements of society. So, what's wrong with that - no drugs, no violence, no pornography?

We have all heard the argument that certain Christian colleges protect their students so much that they are unable to cope with the real world. In fact, I used to believe this. But since working side by side on the mission field with graduates from such colleges, I'd say they have been trained well and can handle the stresses of life. Missionary kids adjust well also.

Perhaps what we need are a few more hot houses in this world, places where children won't be plagued with violence, vice and sex during those very impressionable years. That's exactly what missionary parents have in mind for their children. That's exactly what has produced quality schools for their children around the world.

Staff

The primary and most valuable feature of MK schools are the dedicated Christian personnel, who feel specifically called by God to serve Him in training missionaries' children. Everything else in the schools is secondary to that commitment of raising up children "in the nurture and admonition of the Lord." Teachers and administrators usually are certified by the state or country of their origin. Most of these also have experience in their respective field.

Personnel at missionaries' children schools are generally missionaries responsible to raise their own support. In the Christian and Missionary Alliance schools, the teaching staff is on salary. In the case of a couple sometimes both must teach. Nothing like getting two for the price of one.

Dorm parents have perhaps the most challenging responsibilities.

34

Sometimes it is difficult to know if all their efforts are having any effect on the students. More often than not they may have to await letters from former students to know how it went. Among the letters of this type was one in which a boy stated, "I'm very happy here at Moody Bible Institute. I guess you were right again." He was referring to a statement I had made about his seemingly resisting the Lord and his parents in not wanting to go there.

Facilities

Describing the physical features of MK schools is as difficult as describing schools in any one country. Nevertheless there are a few things that might be stated. First, MK schools are frequently found in the most ideal climate on the field. Since many of the students will be boarding, missionaries tend to select cooler mountain towns, or beach areas where children may enjoy the surroundings.

Some schools are extremely rustic. The dormitories in the first school that I superintended had no windows, only shutters. The siding was unplaned lumber. Inside, rustic, unplaned two by three inch studs stood out as though it were a wood shed or chicken house. Never once did I hear a complaint from the boarders. To this day I believe those students received the best possible education. The summer camp atmosphere is not unusual in MK schools. If there is a choice between buying books or a cement walk, books will be purchased.

On some MK school campuses there are buildings constructed of first class material. These in no way detract from the teaching situation.

It amazes me as I travel what facilities the MK schools do have.
In Sentani, Indonesia, we were privileged to join the students skating
in the gym. The floor is made of iron wood. There is no way that skates
could destroy it. The story was told that a missionary on furlough
asked in a skating rink if they had any old skates for sale. When he
explained why he wanted them, the proprietor stated that the rink had
just acquired new skates and that they could have the old ones as a gift.

Missionaries have become bolder in stating the needs of MK schools,
and Christians have responded with funds for science equipment, tennis
courts, gyms, libraries, swimming pools, computers, projectors and films,
photo laboratories, video cassette recorders, and the list could continue.

Boarding

Most MK schools have boarding facilities. Dormitory population may
number from fifteen to thirty students per unit. Dorm parents are sometimes involved in teaching, coaching, club activities, etc. The ideal situation seems to be that teaching staff not be dorm parents, however some
schools require that teachers perform both tasks. It makes for a very long
day.

It was suggested to us years ago that there are two basic qualifica-
tions for being a missionary: 1, a good sense of humor, and, 2. a bad
sense of smell. In the case of dorm parents we have doubts of survival
for those without humor. A freshman student made our day near the beginning
of first experiences with high school boys. "You'll do fine," he said,
"you have a sense of humor."

On one occasion some senior boys were wrestling in their room.
Sketches of the conversation follow:

Me: "Hey, you guys, why are you wrestling in the dorm? You know
I don't approve of that. Why don't you take your frustrations outside?"

Boy: "You want us to take our frustrations outside?"

Me: "Yea!"

They looked at one another, then at me, and proceeded to pick me up
and carry me outside. Praise the Lord for humor to lighten the way.

The boarding students are usually the "in group." The comradery in
the dorms is strong. Class and student body officers will probably be
boarding students. Sometimes this leads to feelings of being left out by
day students. One mother, sensing this problem with her day students,
told us that she was going to write a book on the problems of day students
who attend boarding schools.

Sponsorship

MK schools often become the center of inter-mission activities. The
diverse doctrines of mission boards tend to separate missionaries, while
the MK schools tend to draw them together. Theological differences may
never be resolved, but educational philosophies within the mission community
tend to be compatible.

School activities such as graduation, plays, musicals and especially
sports draw parents from even remote stations especially if their child is
involved. During these occasions, missionaries who otherwise might not meet,

37

have the opportunity to fellowship and learn to appreciate one another. This is true in schools which are owned and operated by a single mission, as most MK schools are, but perhaps even to a larger extent in the inter-mission schools. Faith Academy in the Philippines is one such inter-mission school and serves over eighty missionary organizations. The self-perpetuating board consists of fifteen people representing fourteen different missions. This school currently enrols over 500 students from kindergarten through twelfth grade. It has three academic buildings, a full size gym, tennis courts, soccer field, covered playground, four on-campus dorms and three off-campus dorms, one with a swimming pool. Two other off-campus dorms are run by individual missions, rather than by Faith Academy. The Faith Academy Association (FAA), a parent-teacher organization, is very active, sponsoring fund raising projects in order to buy new equipment and facilities as well as college scholarships. The FAA may be credited with an increasing awareness among missionaries about one another's ministries and the resulting harmonious relationships.

A veteran staff member at Faith Academy claims that the reason for the school's success is found in its philosophy. It exists primarily to develop the students rather than to meet the needs of the parents. In the process missionaries are served. They are released to give full attention to the task of evangelising the world. In contrast, schools established by individual missions, he feels, have the primary goal of freeing the missionaries in order to meet the goals of those missions. Development of the students may be a secondary goal.

Although there is a lot to consider in this view about inter-mission

38

schools, it is likely that personnel at single mission schools would disagree. Furthermore, they might claim a more unified faculty due to the singleness of doctrine and policies. For example, while most missionaries do not approve of their children dancing, a few mission organizations see it as no problem. Some missions are not opposed to either drinking or smoking in moderation. Therefore we could expect a different set of standards for schools sponsored by them than we would of a more conservative mission school. We would also expect a different doctrinal statement.

Those who expect to send their children to a given school should have a clear understanding of the philosophy, doctrinal position and practices of that school.

The second largest MK school, Rift Valley Academy in Kenya, East Africa, is run by a single mission organization, the African Inland Mission. This school may be credited with bringing together of varying missions. This is true also with the third largest MK school in Quito, Ecuador which is owned and operated by a single organization, the Christian and Missionary Alliance. Like most parents, missionaries want the very best for their children. For them this includes a good education in the Scriptures as well as other subjects which will prepare them for college. To the best of our knowledge, over 90% of the MKs do go on to college. The result has been a curriculum in the MK high schools which has been described as:

"The courses tend to be highly structured and demanding, which may please many parents but turn off their children." (Werkman, 1977)

The fact is that a person·will be hard pressed to find any group of
students more turned on than those we have witnessed in many MK schools.
Granted, studies are not the favorite task of most children, but the MK
seems to be willing to put forth his best effort as though he is doing it
"heartily as to the Lord." (Col. 3:23) It's the motive that counts. For
the missionary child, there is a desire to please the Lord, obey authority,
and honor their parents. In fact, missionaries' children are so conscientious that occasionally an over-zealous teacher who is overloading the
students with work, needs counseling to let up on the requirements.

Apart from the college preparatory courses, there has been an increasing offer of technical and business courses in the last few decades. These
include industrial arts, home economics, photography, aviation ground school,
computer science, and individualized seminars for students with specialized
interests. MK schools are to be commended for the numerous variety of
course offerings in spite of their small size.

<u>Worship</u> <u>Services</u>

Relatively few MK schools take the children to national churches except for special occasions or to minister with programs, such as musicals.
To some this will seem to be a tragedy or a deliberate attempt to avoid
associating with national believers. In response it must be made clear that
the primary objective of missions is to see the national churches run by
nationals and taking large groups of American children to them is not
conducive to an indigenous church.

We have had the privilege of working in schools where we took the stu-

dents to local churches and in others where it was not done. One small
school of twenty-two students went each week to the nearest national church.
We gave the students the equivalent of 5¢ each to put in the offering.
This amount alone frequently made up over one half of the collection. On
occasions when other plans were made for the weekend, the national pastor
seemed offended and hurt by the lack of income for the church.

National church services in this case were conducted in Spanish. That
created another problem for the children whose parents worked in tribal
areas. They were not as conversant in Spanish as in their local dialect.

Then there is a problem of behavior. National teachers are not used
to disciplining American children and some of the MKs take advantage of
them, acting up in class, knowing all the time that the teacher is not
likely to tell the school authorities. To avoid this problem they may
ask the MK school staff members to teach the classes, which sometimes results in lessons designed for the MK more than for the national believers.

MK schools usually are not opposed to the children attending national
churches, but they do believe it works out better for all concerned if
this is done while with their own parents in their respective field of service.

We think we have witnessed the spiritual life slowly dim in MKs who
are required to attend meetings which to them are both long and boring in
national churches. In contrast, we have witnessed MKs come to life under
the ministry of those who understand their needs and are able to apply
scriptural principles to their lives.

Activities

"If you want to stay young, work with young people. If you want to get old in a hurry, try to keep up with them." That advice was given to us by a wise friend before we set foot on foreign soil. We've found it to be exactingly true.

Young people need and enjoy activity. Therefore, their schools provide it. Sports and clubs, gospel and musical teams, plays and speeches. Almost every type of activity found in a Christian school in the States can be found in MK schools. However, they may be modified somewhat. Palm leaves rather than crepe paper may be used to decorate for parties. Clothing may be somewhat less formal at times. Who cares what we look like! We're in the boon-docks.

Most activities thrive because of a staff member's interest and ability to motivate students. In one school the emphasis will be on playing musical instruments, because a teacher who is well liked by the students motivates them. In another school there will be a coach who recognizes ability and is able to form students into winning teams. Some programs come and go with individuals. A ground school aviation course was offered at one location as long as personnel was available.

A few years ago in Tokyo, two MK schools were involved in a regional basketball play off. Other teams such as those from military base high schools were participating. But the unique thing about the two MK teams was that the coach of one was the father of the coach for the other. The son had returned to the mission field to follow the profession of his father, only in a different country.

42

Service and Gospel outreach teams are a part of most MK schools. We have been personally blessed in working with such teams. During one vacation period we had two goals:

1. To discover at least one spiritual gift for each member of the team.

2. To have the privilege of leading at least one soul each to the Lord.

By providing various types of experiences, each member discovered or confirmed a spiritual gift. We had no idea that one girl could teach until she tried it. The children who were generally inattentive were quiet and definitely involved in the lesson when she spoke. The second goal was not readily realized. In fact, we had almost given up when the group was asked to present a service to the patients in a clinic. We weren't going to give an invitation, but at the insistence of the doctor we did. In that moment, the Lord responded with a conversion for each member of the team.

Pre-School

Kindergartens are found in relatively few MK schools. However, many missionaries find that there are neighborhood nurseries, or kindergartens conducted in the national language. Since young children learn so rapidly, it does not take long before they are happily playing with the other children. Parents envy their ability to pick up the language.

These national kindergartens are generally operated by competent well-educated nationals. They provide two key opportunities for the MK:

1. To learn how to get along with other children, and

2. To help them relate to the local culture.

One can imagine the feelings of a missionary who is struggling to learn the language while his pre-schooler is jabbering away in the local dialect.

Some nurseries or kindergartens function in connection with language schools. Young children and parents are both in school during the same time. These schools for children may be run by nationals. Our son, John, attended one such pre-school which was conducted by English speaking Costa Ricans. John was constantly talking about the fun he was having with Mary. From different things he said we finally discovered that Mary was a boy whose actual name was Murray. With the Spanish accent it turns out Mary. We laughed at our new insight and next day shared it with Murray's parents. The mother's face lit up with the information and exclaimed, "Oh, now I know who Joan is. Murray keeps talking about Joan. Joan must be John."

It has been our desire for some time now to compile a list of MK schools. We now think it would be like sweeping water. It would be outdated before it was printed. MK schools follow the missionaries. Old ones close and new ones open. It is therefore suggested that current information be obtained from missions working the country of interest.

NOT FOR EVERYONE

A fifth grade boy was experiencing adjustment problems in a school for missionaries' children. He demonstrated all the symptoms of classical regression (by which is meant a return to earlier stages of development). It was becoming increasingly more difficult for him to get ready for school each morning. He cried easily, was frequently ill, and was losing control of his bowel movements even to the point of soiling his clothes.

His parents came to me for counsel. After they described the symptoms I was convinced that an immediate change of environment was necessary in order to avoid continual regression.

"If he were my child," I stated, "I'd take him out of school for a while."

This was strange advice coming from a person who is so totally sold on schools for missionaries' children. In fact a great amount of my time has been used to encourage parents to believe that their child would do best in an MK school. The truth is still there. The majority of MKs do well in the schools designed for them. However, there are those exceptions which tend to emphasize individual needs.

The parents made the difficult decision to withdraw their son. He was out of school for some months. The results were encouraging. He gained new confidence and the neurotic symptoms fell by the wayside. As can be imagined, the whole family benefited by the change. The following year when he returned to school, he began to experience successes. He was awarded a special recognition by his scout master as the most improved boy in the troop. Improvement continued and he became a recognized leader.

Ordinarily a parent in America would not have the option of withdrawing his child from school for several months. But since there is greater freedom on the mission field for such decisions, it would be beneficial for mission boards to be open to changes. While some mission organizations have policies that state missionaries must send their children to schools run by or recognized by the mission, most groups leave the decision with the parents. There are likely to be problems anytime parents send their children to schools against their own better judgment. If the parents are convinced that a particular educational situation is best, most likely the children will also. The converse is also true.

An eleventh grade missionary boy in a boarding school brought a bottle of gin into the dormitory and drank himself drunk. This boy was not a discipline problem, but seemed to have deep seated emotional problems, the type where one might say "still water runs deep." The dorm parents recommended that he not be readmitted to the dorm for the following school year, not because they could not handle him but because he seemed to need his parents, especially to build a better relationship with his father. Somehow the recommendation was overlooked and the following school year he was once again back in the dormitory.

The dorm parents resolved to do their best for him. What they did

not know was that he had smuggled marijuana into the country in his
guitar. Along with other drugs he sought to meet his own emotional
needs until he was discovered selling drugs to other students. My wife
and I counseled with the parents over a meal one evening. Our hearts
went out to them and their son, but somehow they couldn't grasp the
situation. It was as though they felt God would protect the children of
those serving Him, without them taking a personal interest.

The point I wish to emphasize here is that our children should
take priority over the ministry. If they have needs which will take us
out of His service for a while we need to remember that we are still
performing His will. Remember also I Timothy 5:8: "But if anyone does
not provide for his own, and especially for those of his household, he
has denied the faith and is worse than an unbeliever."

My wife and I are very grateful to the Lord for two outstanding
children who adjusted well to the many changes involved in foreign missionary service. We think one of the keys was our priority for them.
If there had been need to take a year or two out of regular missionary
work to meet their needs we would have gladly done it. In fact, it is a
prerequisite to the ministry to "keep the children under control with
dignity." (I Timothy 3:4)

Some missionaries may seek out the information given here to re-
inforce their misconceptions and misgivings about boarding schools, especially mothers with a strong desire to nurture, provide for and protect their children. Please allow me to point out once again that the
subject here is about exceptional situations. But when a child is ex-

47

periencing adjustment problems the missionary should seek professional help to determine if a change would be advisable.

A first grader was met by her parents at the air strip when she returned from boarding school. Her first words were, "I don't want to go back to school." Imagine what a strong message this was - the first words to her parents after not seeing them for several weeks. After gathering all the facts, once again I recommended that it might be best to keep her home for a semester or two. There was a strong indication that she was not ready for school at the time they sent her. Fortunately there are readiness tests available today which can indicate the advisability of starting a child in school. Age limits alone are not an adequate indication of school readiness, or ability to handle academic matter.

Often parents will feel that their children will be far behind in school if they are the youngest children in their class. Actually in the early grades especially, a month or two of age makes a lot of difference. If in doubt it is generally better to hold a child back and allow him to be at the top of the class rather than struggle at the bottom.

As I have mentioned before my wife and I feel that we have two outstanding children. Our son graduated fifth highest in his high school class. However, when he started first grade he was one of the youngest children in his class. He struggled. His teacher recommended that he be held back. Of course it was a difficult decision to make. But once made he became one of the top students in his grade. I've been able to use this success experience frequently with parents who are struggling with a similar decision.

If a student in any type of educational setting is failing in several areas and is unhappy with school, consider a change. Seek the advice of fellow Christians and especially of those who have the tools and experience to evaluate the situation. We must not assume that God will resolve the problem unless we are willing to allow Him to work through us.

The need for a change of educational environment may surface in all types of situations. If correspondence courses, or national schools, or whatever, are not working out, consider other options. One mother who had successfully taught her children by correspondence courses on the elementary level shared with me that her children had asked to go to a boarding school for their high school years. This frequently happens. The parents must decide. Occasionally a boarding student asks to study at home.

Ordinarily I would advise that students be encouraged to "stick it out" where they are until well adjusted. Nevertheless, there are those unique times where a move is the better choice.

One final word of caution. While it is important to understand how your child feels, it is unwise to let a child make major decisions. Parents sometimes tell their child that he will not be sent to a given school unless he agrees to it. That type of decision is too overwhelming for young children in the elementary grades. On the other hand, parents need to listen more closely to high school students.

The best approach might be to let them know over a period of time that you believe God will provide them with a good education. Then when the decision is made, sit down with the child, look him straight in the eyes and make it very clear that you love him and want the very best for him. Then you may want to say something like, "Your mother and I have prayed about your schooling and considered all the possibilities. We feel that the best situation for next year for you is..." Children need the security of parents who are willing to decide the bigger issues for them. Even though they might resist change, the overall security will help them to make those decisions which they are capable of making.

OTHER EDUCATIONAL OPTIONS

Missionaries predominantly choose to have their children trained in those schools which have been established by mission organizations, specifically for their children. But other options are available. Below are listed these options in what we believe to be the order of use by missionaries. Since no statistics are available, the order is at best an educated guess.

1. International Schools
2. Correspondence or Home Study
3. Mission Schools for Nationals
4. Boarding Schools in the U.S.
5. Boarding with Friends or Relatives in the Home Country
6. Local Public Schools
7. U. S. Department of Defense (DoD) schools
8. Third Language Schools

International Schools

United States Embassy employees and American businessmen may send their children to an international school. These schools, usually located in capital cities, used to be known as American schools. The trend has been to replace "American" with "International."

International schools receive subsidies from the U.S. government, since they enroll so many U.S. citizens. There is an important distinction here in that the federal government does not pay for student tuition as in the schools for military dependents, but funds are available

51

for school use.

The greatest distinction between International School students and MKs is wealth. Embassy employees and businessmen may provide chauffeur driven cars for their children. Furthermore, these children tend to wear more expensive clothes and have more "cold cash" available. An MK attending an International School will sense the peer pressure to "keep up with the Joneses."

In spite of the fact that International schools are heavily subsidized by the U.S. government, tuition is high enough to eliminate many MKs.

A research conducted by Krajewski in 1969 concluded that the dependents of American businessmen were lower academic achievers than the MK or United States government employees' dependents, but claimed the highest self-concept of intellectual ability. On the other hand the MKs were the highest academic achievers of the three groups but had the lowest self-concept of their abilities. One might well imagine the implications of this study for a school where all three classifications of children attend.

Compared to the schools for military dependents, International schools usually have higher academic standards and enroll more non-Americans. It's a status symbol for nationals to be able to send their children to these institutions where instructions are in English.

Missionaries often choose International schools because of their proximity. Rather than sending them off to boarding schools, they may live at home. Naturally most parents prefer to have their children with them as long as they are able to receive a good education. International schools are well equipped and their budgets are enviable. Parents may also like the idea of their children associating with the "higher society" but are not always happy with the peer group value system, which may run counter to Christian standards. Satisfied parents would say, "It's expensive, but worth the sacrifice."

Correspondence Schools or Home Study

The Calvert School is one of the older correspondence schools and used to be the one most frequently used. Before on-the-field schools became available, numerous missionaries used this method. More recently one notices that Missionary Accelerated Christian Education (MACE) is being employed. Many educators in MK schools do not seem to be highly impressed with the quality of this program. Frequently students seem to flounder in regular classes after taking the program. Transcripts are difficult to interpret. For example, 80% appears to be the lowest grade recorded. If a student does less than 80% no score is recorded. He must repeat the course until that percent is earned. Some parents who were under the impression that they would just hand their children the books and tests soon learned that there was a considerable amount of work for them.

Since the MACE courses have been a consecrated effort by dedicated evangelicals to provide a good education for missionaries' children, the expectation is that they will improve with time. Meanwhile, if correspondence courses seem to be the answer, perhaps it would be best to stick with those which are well recognized and accredited, such as the University of Nebraska. Some countries, such as Canada, provide quality correspondence courses free.

A boy in one of the MK schools where we worked had attended several other schools previously. Knowing this, I asked him which was the best school he had ever attended. No doubt my motive was poor, wanting him to respond that his present situation was best.

"I liked studying at home best of all," he emphasized.

"Oh, yes, of course. I had forgotten that you studied at home," I said, "You must have enjoyed being with your mother."

"Well, he said, "it wasn't that so much as the interruptions we had. We'd just get started and someone would knock on the door and mother would dismiss us while she attended them. So we'd go swimming. It happened a lot."

The advantage of correspondence courses is that there is no separation. This usually means more to mother than the child, although she may not realize it. Also, correspondence courses may be used to supplement regular school curriculum.

The disadvantages include the lack of classroom interaction and competition. Correspondence courses seem especially weak in the areas of physical education, laboratory sciences, music and foreign languages. More than one parent using correspondence courses has asked, "How can I motivate my child to do independent study?"

Perhaps the greatest drawback in correspondence courses is the study habits which they seem to produce. Students tend to spend the most time on subjects they like. Furthermore, since there are almost no deadlines, they may procrastinate. After all, if they don't feel ready to take a test today they can do so tomorrow. In the everyday world we are not always blessed with such options.

One of the best ways to determine if correspondence study is the best option is to ask those who have studied by correspondence, rather than those who are currently in it. Ask how it is having mother for a teacher.

For those who go to their field of service with the idea that they will teach their children by correspondence for the first grade or two, I would strongly recommend that they talk to the teachers in the school where the child will eventually be. The foundational or first year is extremely important to any child's development. Some parents have even gone so far as to invite a teacher to live with them on the field for a year or two. This too needs careful planning.

Mission Schools for Nationals

An abundance of overseas schools are run by mission organizations for local citizens. Since they emphasize the Christian philosophy in the classroom they are generally more acceptable to missionaries than the local public schools. Frequently these schools offer instruction in two languages, English in the morning and Spanish in the afternoon, for example. English is the drawing card. Students in these schools are not always happy with what they might call academic pressure.

More than one student has expressed their frustration as one boy did when he said, "You know what my worst subject is? Spanish. I can

55

converse very well but the other students know more than I do. Our
teacher dictates long passages to us, and we lose points for each wrong
letter, punctuation, or capitalization."

Since the school is primarily designed to meet the needs of the
local citizens, instructions tend to be too slow in English and too fast
in the local language for the MK. Occasionally such schools give instruction in three languages, such as Chinese Christian Schools in the Philippines, using Chinese, Tagalog and English. Much of the materials are
learned by rote memory similar to the procedure in the local public
schools.

In spite of the problems or frustrations for MKs in these schools,
many missionaries are able to recount the benefits which their children
derived from them, and will readily recommend the same to others. They
see them as places where their children could establish wholesome relationships with national Christians.

Boarding Schools in the U.S.

Although less common than before the first half of this century,
missionaries sometimes board their children in the U.S. This is true especially on the high school level. Wheaton Academy in Illinois, Taccoa
Falls Academy in Georgia, Markoma Academy in Oklahoma, Ben Lippen Academy
in South Carolina and Hampton-DuBois in Florida, are a few of the schools
frequently used by missionaries. In addition to those boarding schools,
a few missions have boarding homes and send the children to public schools.

Certain missionaries feel strongly about not having teenagers on the field. For girls especially, it can be very trying or tempting when national teenagers shower them with attention. The problem is not necessarily that parents oppose international marriages, although some do. It is actually a cultural problem in societies where premarital sex is the norm. Strange, as I write this, I'm wondering if it isn't already the same in the States now.

A second rationale for sending the high school students to the U.S. is to help them adjust to the current trends, fashions, and philosophies of their fellow countrymen.

The third reason often given is that a quality education cannot be provided on the field. On the elementary level, one teacher is able to teach all subject matter. This is not practical on the secondary level. A team of teachers is required. Also a school needs to be a certain size before one can justify particular facilities and equipment, such as science laboratories, and computers. Sports events are also in need of a certain number of participants. This would include competing teams from other schools.

Therefore boarding schools in America have been able to provide a well rounded education for the MK and they may continue to do so. However, parents, as has been stated, prefer to keep their children close to them on the field. High schools with excellent equipment and staffs have proven themselves on foreign soil. Having the students close enough to be able to visit with them occasionally is a morale booster to parents and children alike.

Boarding with Friends or Relatives in the Home Country

Missionaries have, on occasion, found the best solution for their children's education was to leave them with friends or relatives in the country of citizenship. This is much more common on the high school than the elementary school level.

Grandparents have been good candidates for this task. However, one needs to keep in mind the gap which might exist between the two generations.

Aunts and Uncles have functioned well as surrogate parents. They would be closer in age to the actual parents than the grandparents and their philosophy of child rearing may be close to that of their brother or sister. The same may be true of friends. These friends may have grown up or attended college with the missionaries. They may be members of a supporting church. In the latter case, the church may become involved.

Missionaries have looked upon these arrangements as closer to the ideal. Their children will share a home rather than a dormitory. Though there will be rules and standards, these will not demand as close adherence as they might in a dormitory. Meal schedules and lights out may shift more readily, for example.

In the case of boarding schools in the home country, there may be longer lapses for the MK between visits with their parents. This could be as long as four years during a regular term of missionary duty.

Mission organizations have been known to provide funds for students to travel to the field every year or two. On the other hand, missionaries have sometimes sacrificed their meager savings for such occasions.

Local Public or National Schools

One missionary couple working in a small Central American republic
chose to send their two sons to a local Spanish speaking school. There
were no boarding schools in the country at the time. Soon after we were
privileged to establish a boarding school, these boys were enrolled. They
were friendly and full of drive. The faculty enjoyed working with them
in spite of the academic problems. Their general intelligence scores on
written IQ tests were very much below average, due to the language barrier.
Nevertheless, we knew they were intellectually above average. They were
fluent in conversational English but read and wrote little besides Spanish.
During one vacation the boys wrote us. The letter was something like this:

"Dir Uncul Dan and Ant Luis,

I em having a gud vacashun an mis u an evrybody at eschul."
Some sections of the letter would have been virtually impossible for us
to read if we did not know Spanish. Fortunately, these boys will do well
in U.S. or in Latin America because of their outgoing and friendly personality. But more than likely they will continue to struggle with written
English.

A high school student who enrolled in an MK boarding school in the
eleventh grade was ridiculed for his strong identification with the national culture. The boys would accuse him of all sorts of things, such
as not flushing the toilet. "He's just like a beak. They never flush the
toilets," they would say. The word beak was the derogatory word which some
used for nationals. Such statements were both inaccurate and cruel. He
was totally rejected by those who thought themselves to be better. Finally,

he did break into the group by means of karate. He brought a national friend to the school to teach this skill. One evening the instructor placed this boy in the front of the group, and asked the others to come one at a time to try and throw him. One after another they came and were thrown to the mat. He had gained acceptance. Nevertheless, he still carries the psychological scars received from the rejection of his identity with nationals.

If the object were for missionaries' children to become citizens of the country in which their parents work and continue living there, there would be no more reasonable way to educate them than to do so in the schools of the country involved. But since this is not generally so, the task is to equip the children for adjustment in the country of their citizenship.

On the other hand, there are outstanding success stories of students who spent the first few years in local schools, studying in the national language and later transferred to American schools. One such girl shared that when she was young she considered herself to be 90% Filipino and 10% American. Soon after starting in an MK boarding school she felt that she was half Filipino and half American. Finally, in her last years in high school she considered herself 90% American and 10% Filipino. She was selected by the faculty to be the outstanding Senior girl.

So we conclude that some can with effort make the transfer from one language and culture to another, but others struggle and do not tot-

ally change. Although no statistics are available, we sense that there
are more casualties than successes in these instances.

Most MKs are fluent in both English and at least one foreign
language, but very few become totally literate in both. Public schools
in areas where missionaries work may have larger classes, sometimes fifty
or sixty students, and less well equipped than in the United States. The
teacher may dictate or have students copy the subject matter from the
board. There may not be any books, maps or library. The teachers must
be stern or firm in order to handle so many students. One MK was punished
by having to stand and stare at the sun. Another had to kneel on mango
beans (a bean-sized seed) for long periods of time.

It may be that for these reasons relatively few missionaries choose
to send their children to national schools.

Since educational standards have been on the upward trend around
the world, it might be time for missionaries and mission boards to re-
evaluate the policy of not training the dependents in national schools.
At the same time, it might be that the reasons missionaries have tended
to shy away from such schools still exist.

Department of Defence Schools (DoD)

Schools especially designed for the education of American Military
personnel's children are found in strategic locations around the world.
The majority of larger U.S. military installations host such schools. The
facilities are usually equipped with the most up-to-date educational tools.
The faculty members are well trained and receive above average salaries.

61

The well-kept bases, with mowed lawns, shops and recreational facilities are known as "little Americas."

Occasionally, non-military dependents are allowed to attend these schools. The advantages are that a student might be able to stay at home with his parents if they live near a DoD school and receive a well-rounded education in a well equipped school rather than go to a boarding school.

The disadvantages from the missionaries' standpoint would include the lack of spiritual training along with the peer pressures which generally would oppose the Christian ethic. To service men the term "military brat" is assigned to military service personnel's children. Although the word "brat" does not apply to most of these students, as a whole they do differ from MKs. Research has indicated them to be not as highly intelligent, but more outgoing than MKs. Uncertainty is a part of the serviceman's lot. Until recently most moved at least every two or three years. The terms of service in a particular location tend to be lengthening. However, the families do not have the privilege of knowing very far in advance where they will be assigned. Students may have to plant roots in a second school in any given year. This mobility differs greatly from the MK who can probably tell you exactly where he will be several years in advance. The mobility means that in a DoD school, students do not usually develop long term friendships.

Another possible concern to the missionary would be lower academic standards. For example, graduation requirements in the DoD high schools include only one science and one math course. Fifteen is the total number of credits required for graduation in contrast to 21 in some MK schools.

Nevertheless, some missionaries have benefited from DoD education for their children. They might agree with the parents of children in International schools that the expenses are high but worth the sacrifice. If enrollment of missionaries' children in DoD schools were not so limited, more might attend them.

Third Language Schools

In some capital cities one may find a school which teaches not in English nor the local language but in a third language such as German. These schools are meant to provide an education for embassy employees and business men from other nations.

Occasionally missionaries use these schools. One family sent a daughter and son to a German school for a while. The parents were natural linguists. At home they would choose days in which they would converse only in German, and other days only in Spanish. Since the two oldest children were exceptionally bright, they handled it well. But the third child did not seem to enjoy it as much and the parents found it necessary to change their approach in his case.

It would be my recommendation not to submit a child to such rigorous training unless there is a very definite aptitude in that area. The problem is that most of us like to believe that our children are brighter than the general population (of course they are). We like to feel that they can excel in all areas. A competent professional would be able to identify the aptitudes and interests of children, and recommend the areas and extent to which an individual is likely to excel.

Conclusions?

So after all the above one still may ask, "Which educational option is best for missionary kids?" The answer is, as a child might say, "It depends."

It depends on the parents' attitude.

It depends on what schools are available.

It depends on finances.

It depends on the ability of the children.

It depends on the childrens' ages.

It depends on mission policy.

It depends on what God has in mind, and knowledge of that usually comes by personal time in prayer and in the Word, along with counsel of fellow missionaries.

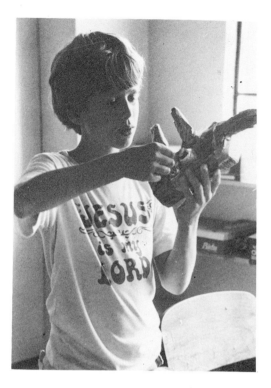

MK schools such as
Faith Academy encour-
age students to dis-
cover and develop
their talents. An art
student (left) ex-
presses himself.
Below, high school stu-
dents jest at pushing
a school bus, but some-
times it's no joke.

Mr. Don Boesel, Superin-
tendent, congratulates
a senior upon her
graduation (right).
It is not unusual for
MKs to learn to play a
musical instrument at an
early age (below).

In some MK schools,
virtually every stu-
dent takes instrumen-
tal music lessons.
There are ample oppor-
tunities for Faith
Academy students to
perform in local chur-
ches, evangelistic en-
deavors, and in school
assemblies.

In addition to musical
performances (below)
Faith Academy, like
many larger MK schools,
has an extensive sports
program. Over 80% of
the F.A. high school
students participate in
some sport, such as
basketball (left) and
cross country (below
left).

Ed and Louise Danielson
with the Timothy Teams
which they directed.
These traveled in the
Philippines during the
vacation months of 1976
(above) and 1977 (right).
They cooperated with the
local churches in evan-
gelism and physical labor.

In 1970, a typhoon
named Yoling destroyed
over 50% of the build-
ings at Faith Academy.
Christians around the
world responded with
offerings for the
restoration which
lasted for over a year.

Ed Danielson as a dorm parent in 1970 (above), and
as the high school counselor in 1975 (below).

Elementary students at Faith Academy, enjoying the library (left).

Faith Academy students distributing tracts and witnessing (right). One of the students' favorite places to evangelize is in Rizal Park near the Manila Bay.

PREPARING THE MISSIONARY CHILD

Woody was about 12 years old when we first met him in Managua.
We had been driving down the Pan American highway on our way to language school in Costa Rica. Since my Spanish was limited at the time,
Woody was my guide and interpreter. On the way to the telegraph office he began almost immediately to tell me about the boarding school
which he attended in Honduras. The conversation went something like
this:

Woody: "Guess what. Next week we get to go back to Las Americas"
        (the boarding school)

Me: "And you are looking forward to it?"

Woody: "Yes, we sure are. Have you ever been there?"

Me: "No. What's it like?"

Woody: "Well, there is a river which runs through the property and
        we get to go swimming in it every day. It is a big farm with
        horses, and sheep, and chickens, and geese, and rabbits, and
        all kinds of fruit trees, oranges, mangoes, lemons, grapefruit,
        papayas and bananas. There is so much land there that a per-
        son can get lost."

Obviously, Woody was as excited as a child on his first trip to
Disneyland. He continued talking about the many wonderful attributes
of Las Americas, the property, the buildings, the staff and students.
I only wish that everyone who has ever doubted the advisability of MK
boarding schools could have witnessed this boy expounding on a very
important part of his life.

65

My own impression went something like this, "Hey, this kid really enjoys boarding school." We had been told of the many good features of the two MK schools in Central America, but in the back of my mind I had suspected that the children must look upon them as second best, and that they had learned to happily endure the situation. At the time we didn't know that the Lord would have us working in that school a year later. He certainly was preparing our hearts for the work.

Preparation for School

Woody's parents were successful missionaries. Their ministries had been fruitful. Their children were dedicated and secure in their love and considered their educational experiences to be a part of their parents' loving provision for them. They stood on the philosophy of "We know not what the future holds, but we know who holds the future." The best possible situation is for every missionary to truly dedicate houses, brothers, sisters, fathers, mothers, children and fields (Matt. 19:29) to the Lord, entrusting all of these to Him. That leaves the door wide open for God to work. "With man this is impossible, but with God all things are possible." (Matt. 19:26)

In recent years it seems that we are witnessing more and more young couples going into foreign service stating that they will never send their children away. That works out fine as long as they don't find it necessary to. One of the hardest types of counseling cases is a child who is in boarding school after being continually told that he would never be sent away. The child feels deceived, and his entire system of values which he has acquired from his parents will doubtlessly be altered under the circumstances.

Similar to the way in which Woody's parents had been successful in missionary outreach, they had done an outstanding job of preparing their children for school. First of all they believed that God really does meet all our needs "according to His riches in Glory." (Phil. 4:19) They believed it so strongly that their children sensed it.

A child properly prepared for school has parents who are properly prepared. These parents are open and honest with their children. They may not be able to say exactly where a child will study, but they can always assure them that God will provide for them in wonderful ways.

Once it is clearly established where a child will study, the parents should make the situation very clear to them, and build up the positive aspects of the school. A discussion of the feelings one experiences when separated is necessary but should not be overworked.

Actually, hundreds of missionaries have successfully handled the strong emotions accompanying the sending of children to boarding school. They realize that the situation would provide the maximum of advantages for their children.

Leaving the MK at school

One year after meeting Woody, I was installed as director of Las Americas. I learned how successful missionaries leave their children at school. The procedure goes like this. An activity is planned for the child and the parents simply say that they will be leaving while the child is doing so and so. An older brother or sister, a dorm parent or a former student will take the new student to see the chickens, or for

67

a swim with other students. Getting in a circle and praying generally
adds stress to the situation. Mother will perhaps be the first to
break down in tears and the children will soon join in. Pray, yes, but
"watch and pray." The children have already prayed numerous times with
the parents about school and they have been assured that Mother and Dad
will remember them every day before the Lord.

There are no doubt individuals who, in the name of psychology,
would claim the above procedure to be unhealthy, a repression of true
feelings. The fact is that the process is suppression, a conscious control of feelings, a very healthy approach to situations such as leaving
a child in boarding school. There is no denial of strong feelings, just
a proper way to work with them.

Missionary parents sometimes feel that staying in the area of the
boarding school for a week or so helps the children adjust. The reality
is that such a practice sometimes hinders adjustment. The children seem
to be confused as to who is really in charge. Some will show symptoms
of homesickness. One older student put it this way, "My brother (younger)
will do fine as soon as my parents go back home. As long as they are
here he thinks maybe there is a chance that he can go home with them."
His statement was prophetic. The very day his parents left, the brother
began to fit into the dorm and school with no problems. It seems that
when the parents stay in the area, they are expressing some doubts about
the welfare of their children and may actually be dealing with some feelings of guilt.

Security at School

We have found that it works well for children to be in class when the parents leave after a visit. On one occasion the parents of a first grade boy requested that we take him out of class so they could say goodbye. As they stood there the mother broke down into tears, followed by her son. They prayed together, gave him a very expensive toy and left. It was difficult to console the boy. In my efforts to do so I said, "Wow, that's a nice truck they gave you." His only response was sobs. Then I said, "You have a wonderful father." "I'm not so sure," he responded. "Well, you certainly have a wonderful mother," I continued. "I don't know about that either."

Of all the children in the school, he was the only one who seemed unhappy. We discussed this with his parents at a later date. The problem as they saw it was not the school, but the insecurity their son felt. They related all he had been through before coming to the school. We all were convinced that his basic insecurity seemed to be with him at home as well as at school. As the school year progressed he became secure with the surroundings and daily routine. We can only hope that some of his new-found security followed him into his home.

From this early experience we gleaned a principle which time has verified: Children who are secure in their home, will be secure in a boarding school. Furthermore, a child who is not secure at home, may be able to establish security in the school, but this will not be quite the same as security with the parents.

The First Grader

Preparing the child for first grade involves much more than it
does for the following grades. There is no good reason that we know of
why a child should be sent to school before six years of age. We have
observed a trend toward getting children started early. The U.S. Department of Health, Education and Welfare was involved in the Head Start
Program in which thousands of pre-school children were gathered in
schools for the purpose of preparing them for future education. One
research indicated that there seemed to be very little evidence that
these children actually did do better in school than they would have
without such a head start.

An MK school board once voted to not allow any child in the boarding units until he was six years old. It was my dubious privilege as
chairman of the board to withstand the verbal responses of parents on
this matter. At the time the ruling was established, I did not realize
that two families would be affected.

The parents of one child were not in the least happy. As the
father stated it, he and his wife were looking forward to working together in the Lord's work with their last child in boarding school, and
now that would not be possible.

The second set of parents had a child who missed the deadline by
two days. Their approach was much different. They accepted the decision as from the Lord. They were actually looking forward to having
their son with them one more year before going to school.

If there is some doubt as to the child's being ready for boarding school, or even regular school, professional help may be considered. The effort to have a child tested ahead of time can be most self-assuring. Schools should have readiness tests which require very simple tasks, such as drawing squares and circles and answering simple questions orally. These tests should be administered by someone other than the parents or close friends. The reason for this is to discover how the child will do in a new situation.

Regarding boarding school, below are listed a few tasks which a student should be able to do by himself:

1. Put on and button, zip or tie clothes.
2. Tie shoes.
3. Comb own hair.
4. Make a bed.
5. Take a shower or bath without help.
6. Pick up clothes and put them away.
7. Respond when spoken to.
8. Take care of his own toilet.
9. Eat at least a little of everything set before him and drink milk.

The above check list would seem to be a little more than necessary for going to a day school, and rightly so. House parents tend to be cordial and helpful. But few of them are able to comb 20 or more heads of hair, or tie forty shoes, each morning.

If the child is a bed wetter, inform the dorm parents and plan to provide plastic pads for under the sheets.

We have recommended to numerous parents to see if they couldn't send their child ahead of time for an overnight stay in the school. This works best if an older brother, sister or friend is there. If the school is not able to do this, arrangements should be made to let him stay at some other mission station for a day or two. Some children have never been away from mother until the first day in an MK school. This does not have to be. One may plan ahead. Perhaps the house parents will be willing to have a child stay with them for a day or so during the vacation period. Please, this suggestion should be handled carefully. If nineteen other children's parents want to do likewise, the house parents may not have the vacation which they deserve. Remember, there is no more demanding job than being parents to a household of children. Which reminds me of something the missionary parents can do to help. They may offer to take charge of the dormitory for an evening or two while they are visiting the school sometime.

A list of instructions will be helpful to the house parents who, being normal, may not remember all the special instructions on the day the boarding unit is opened. They will want to know of any special health or behavioral problems. Also it is wise to leave wrapped presents for any special occasions such as birthdays that will occur while the MK is at school. It might not be wise to depend on postal services to deliver them on time.

It has amazed us to notice the difference between the children whose parents seem to leave a superabundance of detailed instructions and those who simply say, "If he gives you any trouble feel free to spank him." We can't remember that an MK of the latter type ever had to be spanked. The secret must be in the support which the parent gives the houseparents.

The High School Student

In the case of older children, our strongest message is don't take a high school student to the mission field unless he is willing to go. Changing high schools is always difficult, so why add the problems of foreign residence. At school he may not feel accepted. After all, the other MKs have much more in common. They know local customs and probably speak the language of the area.

If the high school student had stayed in his home country, he might be driving but may not be able to on the field, either because of local laws or lack of a vehicle.

Home to the MK is the field while to a new arrival it is probably America. An MK was having an argument with his father about a minor problem. Finally he said in disgust, "Oh, you wouldn't understand it anyhow." "Try me," the father said. "Well," he began, "you like the States because that's home to you. You grew up there. But I grew up on the mission field, so that's home to me."

It may be worth the try to talk a teenager into going to a foreign country for a short term of perhaps six months to a year, before their senior year. The experience may give them a good understanding of how others live. It must be remembered, however, that they may have to give up a boyfriend or girlfriend, their gang, a job, even their freedom to travel around by themselves. In some areas of the foreign field it is

73

not advisable to travel alone. Their diet will be different. There may not be any ice cream or hamburgers or pop available, items which are important to most teenagers. The climate may differ drastically from their hometown.

The probability of successful adjustment of a teenager going to the mission field for the first time may be measured with one simple question: "What do you think of your parents going overseas?" Who asks this and how it is asked is very important. A boy of whom I asked this question in the U.S. stated that he thought it was a good idea and acted excited about leaving. Unfortunately, I was not able to talk to him alone, and did not pursue the subject further. When we later met overseas, I reminded him of his response, and he stated that he felt he couldn't give his true feelings in front of his parents. His adjustment was difficult.

Children must also be prepared for the types of clothes they might be expected to wear in boarding schools. The difference in dress between tribal areas and the city may be considerable. Schools will be glad to supply a list of the clothes and other items needed. It is suggested that such lists be requested well in advance in order to allow time to purchase those things which are not at hand.

Missionaries need special wisdom in preparing their children for school. Fortunately, the Lord freely offers His wisdom to those who ask. (James 1:5)

The Pre-School MK

The two year old son of a young couple in language school was playing with some small cars in front of the house. He began crying for no reason that could be detected. There were no indications of injury or bites and he was not running a temperature. Since this same type of thing had happened several times before, the parents began to review the situation. They had just recently moved to the field. The house was new. The climate was different than what they had before. His vocabulary and ability to speak were above average for his age - in English, but the house girl spoke only Spanish. Church services were in Spanish. The parents spent all morning in language school and studied much of the afternoon. They owned no car, so traveled by public transportation. The diet was different.

The only logical solution was for the mother to be with him instead of going to school. She would take classes in the afternoon by a tutor. The change worked wonders. A mission representative agreed with the change saying, "You'll get the language later, but you may never make up for this time that you need to be with your son."

Before one year of age, children seem to adjust well. They aren't speaking yet and consider all adults as much the same. Then again after the child is in a kindergarten or nursery, adjustment seems to go smoothly. Therefore, the critical time is between one and five years of age. This has been verified over the years. It seems advisable for mothers to spend as much time as possible with the children during these ages. If language school is imperative, it would be helpful to organize a cooperative nursery so that children may have the security of companions with similar backgrounds.

Pre-Field Preparations

The MK needs constant reassurance that everything is under control during the whirlwinds of deputation and packing. There is little hope of actually being able to convey to the pre-schooler what is happening or what is about to take place. Their assurance that everything is fine will come from parents' time and attention. The tendency may be to over-do it and perhaps overprotect or spoil the child. Wise missionaries plan to have favorite toys readily available as one way to help continuity. Love and affection are important, but discipline for unacceptable behavior should continue as a stabilizing effect.

For the elementary student, parents should explain exactly what is happening and when it will happen, as much as possible. It is not wise to allow a young child to have a part in the choice. For a child to have to choose between his best friend who he plays with every day and the Lord in the tropics, whom he has never seen, is a bit overwhelming. His level of enthusiasm will probably reach that of his parents. He needs assurance that he will make new friends. The MK will benefit from an emphasis on the positive aspects of foreign living, such as animals, plants and terrain.

It is well for missionaries to remember that very few children have the opportunity to have a voice in where father or mother will work.

In packing for the field, children need to be assured that if there is something very important to them which cannot be shipped, that it will be put in storage to await their return for furlough.

MAINTAINING CONTACT WITH THE MK IN BOARDING SCHOOL

Visits to the School

As we look back over the years of observing parents visit schools
and remember the times when we visited our own children, many fond memo-
ries fill our minds.

On one occasion the staff was happy to put us to work when we
visited our children who were at that time enrolled in boarding school.
We hiked, and swam, read to the students and led them in devotional
thoughts and Sunday services. You don't have to talk much to get permission to take the dorm kids off on a weekend hike. House parents are
glad for the break. We chose to have a blind rope hike one night. The
students were lined up, blindfolded, and given a place to hold on a
long rope. We then led them out into the woods and every so often tap-
ped one on the shoulder. That was a signal to stop, count to 500, take
the blindfold off and try to find their way back to the school. They
loved it!

A Christmas film we had brought from the capital was shown on the
eve of Easter. That was the only one available, and no one objected.

On the last day of that particular visit it was my privilege to
give the Easter Sunday message. Several students were saved that day,
and adults took them aside to counsel them. In the dormitory later one
girl was found in tears. "I wanted to be saved when Uncle Dan spoke,"
she sobbed. The dorm parent explained that she could do it right then
and had the privilege of leading her to Christ.

We recall observing other parents visiting their children in schools

77

where we were working. They shared with students and staff about the struggles and victories of their missionary work. Some parents were particularly good story tellers, perfect for addressing students around a camp fire. Others liked to get a ball game going, or helped the students with hobbies. Everyone seemed to benefit, dorm parents, students, and parents.

Special events at school such as sports, dramatic productions, or musicals, present excellent opportunities for parents to be with their children. Missionaries may be the most involved individuals when it comes to the education of their children, and therefore do not pass up these events if they can help it.

Keeping that in mind, we might ask about how it affects children who are not visited during these peak experiences. Our observations suggest that most of them take it very well. A few, however, will make revealing statements such as, "I've lettered in basketball for four years now, and my parents have never seen me play." This sometimes happens to day students as well as boarders. The boarders, of course, don't expect their mother and father to attend all activities.

We recommend that parents attend as many school sponsored activities as possible. For boarding school parents, arrangements should be made to visit the school at times when there is an important event for their child. This may be a leading part in the senior play, a championship game of soccer in which he is involved, an art festival when he has something on display, or such occasions.

Listed below are a few suggestions for missionaries visiting their

78

children in boarding school:

1. Get involved with the children in the same types of activities which are enjoyed at home.

2. Don't spend time "sermonizing" as the children might call it. In most cases they already know what you believe, how you feel and what you expect from them. If they don't already know that you love them they won't learn it in a sermon while you visit them.

3. Emphasize the positive: how glad you are that God has provided such a wonderful school, a caring staff, etc.

4. Play down the disadvantages. Parents sometimes make the error of repeating over and over again how much they miss their child, how lonely it is at home and how glad they will be to have them home again.

5. Spend time alone with the child when he chooses, not when the parent desires. Situations such as this arise from time to time: A parent arranges for a picnic lunch to take their child away from school one afternoon. The child goes, but later lets it slip that he was going to be the pitcher for the ball game that afternoon.

6. Visit the classrooms if the child requests it, otherwise be very cautious. Some children are embarrassed to have their parents in their classes.

7. Take them reasonable gifts only, such as something you have made. Remember you are what they really want, not gifts.

8. Be cautious about showering them with junk food. If you must bring something to eat, bring enough to share with everyone and ask the

dorm parents what is the best way to distribute it. It is sad to see a child hide a can of goodies, and get into it only while others are not around. The child seems to be learning selfishness and may think that his parents believe that the school does not feed him properly.

9. Offer to help the school staff. Parents often speak in chapels or devotions, teach classes, do maintenance work, or relieve the dorm parents for an evening.

10. Stay at the dorm overnight only if invited by the dorm parents and then for three days at the most. Dormitory students are like any other children in that visitors to the home for long periods of time may disrupt the routine. A room near by may be the better situation. Many dorms do not have guest rooms.

11. Don't be hurt if it seems like you are being ignored. This usually indicates that your child is well adjusted and you should be encouraged. It's the child who clings to his parents all the time they are visiting that is suffering from insecurity.

Correspondence

If we put ourselves in the place of the MKs away at boarding school we can imagine what they would not want in letters. They don't want instructions of how to behave, they get that all day long. They aren't in need of Dad's sermons, they've heard most of them already. They don't need to be told how or what to eat, the aunts and uncles tell them all the time. They don't need to hear about every cold or fever the family has, they can't do too much about it, and it will probably be cured before the letter arrives.

Here's a good example of a poor letter:

Dear Joe,

Your father and I have had a bad cold for three weeks now and don't seem to get much done. But I did want to let you know that we miss you more and more every day. Yesterday I was in your room and started to cry when I realized we won't see you for another month.

Don't forget to take your vitamins every morning and brush your teeth after every meal. Dentists are expensive today and we aren't rich, you know.

Are you still reading your Bible and praying every day? Remember, a verse a day keeps the Devil away.

How are you doing in math? We noticed that you got a C+ last time. Some colleges won't accept students with less than a B average.

We can hardly wait until you come home. I'm already planning to have a special meal for you. Just let me know what you'd like that you don't get at school.

Be good! We love you and miss you very much.

Love,

Mother

P.S. Hi, son, this is Dad. I just wanted to caution you about playing with sling shots, even if Uncle Bob thinks it's o.k. A stone from a sling shot can travel very fast and do a lot of damage. You might put somebody's eye out and would regret it the

rest of your life. I'd like to write more but I have to
get ready for the service tonight.

Love,

Dad

Letters from home are usually a highlight for the MK boarder.
It's sad to see the reaction of children who receive letters like the
above. We have actually seen them setting around, unopened for days.
We have asked, "Aren't you going to read your letter?" and they respond,
"Oh, yea, later," and run off to play.

In contrast there are parents whose letters are so interesting
that other students and dorm parents want to read them. An example is
given:

Dear Mary,

You remember the red and yellow bird we watched make a
nest in the tree in the back yard before you left for school?
Well, there are three little baby birds there now. It's funny
to see how they crane their necks and open their mouths. The
mother crams worms and bugs down their gullets, and their
bellies become.round and bulging, with all that food.

Every morning I pick some beans from the bushes you planted.
We've already canned twelve jars full of them. Jerry helps me
in the garden. It's fun to watch him tug at the weeds. He's
not old enough to do as well as you do.

Dad has gone on another evangelistic trip. Don Nago from
next door has gone with him. We think he's about ready to trust

Christ. Doña Maria, his wife, accepted the Lord last week.
So our prayers are being answered. Their daughter Nila enjoys the bicycle that you loaned her while you are at school.
Sometimes she comes to help us in the garden. She also
helps me get the flannelgraph lessons for the children's class
each week. She asked me to say "Hola" to you in my next
letter.

We pray for you every day and know that God is blessing
you.

Please give our love to Uncle Jim, and Aunt Joan.

Love,

Mother

Children enjoy drawings and photos in their letters also.

Once a week is about the right frequency. Every day becomes too
common and less than once a week is too infrequent. Usually the students
are required to write home once a week. If you have more than one child
at school, each one deserves his own personal letter. If it takes too
long because you have too many children, consider putting one or more up
for adoption. Dad should not leave all the letters to Mother. Children
want to hear from him also.

Letters are not always assured of speedy and dependable delivery
on the mission field. Some letters may be lost in transit. Therefore,
do not assume something is wrong if you don't receive one. Parents should
consider sending telegrams for special occasions since they are usually
inexpensive overseas.

Another "No No" for missionaries is correcting the child's letter and returning it. Grammar and spelling should never overshadow communication. We are aware of one parent who made big red corrections on her son's letter. To this day there is some difficulty for him as an adult in writing to her.

Many missionaries have received letters like this:

Dear Mom and Dad,

As you know we have to write letters to our parents in order to get Sunday night supper. I'm in a hurry, so this is mine.

Love,

Jerry

This type of letter should not startle the parent. It probably means all is well and does not deserve a reprimand in your next letter. If it happens every week, however, there may be a problem.

One parent received the usual short weekly letter from their son. Sons aren't usually given to letter writing as much as daughters. At the end of the letter there was a P.S.:

"Oh, I forgot to tell you, I was in the hospital last week, but I'm o.k. now.

Love,

John."

No further details were included.

Children have been known to write very startling letters to parents, even to the point of expressing hate for the school and asking the parents to come and get them right away. In the majority of these cases the feelings are temporary. They may have had a fight with their best friend or got a failing grade on one test. In a day or two they will probably feel completely different. After all, they are children.

Personally we made a practice of always writing each letter in such a way that we wouldn't mind others seeing it. We still believe that is the best policy, although there may be rare exceptions. We suggest that missionary prayer letters be sent the children and staff.

Authority

In keeping with Scriptural principles we desire to help children recognize the value and importance of obeying authority. Let us remember that we do not generally have sadistic teachers nor houseparents who love to beat children and put them to bed each night without food. Since they are professing Christians, parents will find it advantagious to support and not undermine them. Even when we feel they are wrong we have the opportunity to counsel our children to learn how to cope with it.

Our daughter once asked permission to drop a class. There was a clash between her and the teacher. The teacher seemed to have a problem in getting along with people in general. I bought up the opportunity to challenge our daughter. "If you can figure out how to get along with her and please her, you will have learned a valuable lesson," I said, "There will be many more people like her throughout life with whom you'll work."

She accepted the challenge and became the teacher's favorite student.

When it does seem necessary to confront a staff member, it is best done in private with that person, never in front of the child.

Small gifts or notes of thank you are always welcomed by those working at the school. It truly is the thought and not the value that counts. They, like other missionaries, have given up a few things in order to support the missionary endeavor.

WHAT BOARDING SCHOOLS DO TO MISSIONARIES' CHILDREN

For over 25 years now, my wife and I have been privileged to observe missionaries' children in boarding schools. We've followed their
development and adjustment to the demands of our modern world. Each time
we return to the U.S. we find that we have to assure Christians that MK
schools are doing a good job.

Ask an MK who has been in a boarding school how he liked it.
Chances are that he's been asked that question numerous times. He may
smile and respond that it was a good experience. He already knows what
the next question will be, "Didn't you miss your father and mother?" His
response will be, "Yes, I missed them, but it was the best way for me to
get a good education." Actually, he probably gets a little perturbed with
these standard questions but he will be polite and give his honest response.
There are standard statements that he also puts up with while on furlough.
People will say to his parents in his presence, "I could never send my
children off to a boarding school," with the implication that the individual must think he loves his children more than the missionaries love theirs.

As part of a three day presentation on MK schooling before two to
three hundred missionaries studying Spanish in Costa Rica, we had a panel
of one second generation MK, an MK, a teacher in an MK school, and the
parent of an MK in a boarding school. The meeting was opened to questions.
A father primed the MK prior to his question by saying, "Now forget all the
instructions which you were given in advance and just tell us what you don't
like about the boarding school."

In jest, I feigned like he might be ruining us with such a question, by putting my hand to my forehead and moaning. Laughter filled the auditorium, but I had reason to regret the act. After what I had done it was difficult for those present to think anything but that I had given him strict guidelines. Actually all I had said to him was to give honest answers.

After thinking for a while, the MK was not able to name anything that he didn't like about the school and stated so. Here was a very articulate brilliant boy who had answered so many questions well, and was not able to think of one negative thing about an entire school.

After the meeting he volunteered to me that he had tried very hard but couldn't think of a thing. Suddenly he remembered something, "I've thought of something," he said, "we can't have seconds on desserts."

To this day, I suspect, there are those who felt it was a rigged meeting.

Frequently I have shared the ministry of MK schools in U.S. churches. During a question session in one Sunday School class, a mother asked, "How young are the youngest children in the boarding schools?" I knew where she was going when I responded "six years old." It seemed as though she were close to tears when she asked if they didn't miss their parents. Let me make it clear, first of all, that MK boarding schools are not like the proverbial orphanages in literature where children are undernourished, overworked, and beaten. As a whole, the MK school is staffed with dedicated Christians, who consider their job to be a calling of God, and are supportive of the parents' ministries.

Perhaps you know of exceptions. We are not blind to these. In fact,

88

we could relate a few tragic stories about MKs and MK school staff. Several years ago, Louise, my wife, and I were invited to work in a certain boarding school. The ones who wrote us stated, "We love the kids, but our hearts are really with the Indians where we have worked."

It begins something like this. A missionary conference is held on the field. Someone brings up the need for a school for the children of the missionaries. Some mothers may be teaching their children with correspondence courses which frequently does not work out well. Others may be sending theirs to the national schools, only to realize that their children are not learning English as well as they should and the courses do not include subjects required for enrollment in American colleges. The missionary conference members agree that they should establish a school on the field. Then there comes the decision as to who will work in the school. Since there seems to be an urgency to start, a missionary already on the field is asked to fill in "just for a year." Unfortunately, the group may select the ones who are not experiencing success in their present ministry. They may skip over the best talent such as a couple having an outstanding ministry with youth groups. They cannot be spared, so it would seem. This story could be repeated many times over for various places in the world. MKs can see right through it. They know when they have dorm parents and teachers who "love them" while their hearts are with the Indians.

MKs also sense a difference between short term teachers or dorm parents and career missionaries. One MK suggested to me that the high percentage of faculty members who come for only one year was the reason for problems within the student body. "It's as though they aren't really interested in us," she said.

During one furlough I asked three questions of many groups to whom I spoke:

1. How many of you would be willing to serve the Lord full time, if you knew He wanted you to? (response - about 80%)

2. How many would be willing to serve the Lord overseas, if you knew He wanted you to? (response - about 50%)

3. How many of you would be willing to send your children to boarding schools, if you knew it was God's will? (response about 10%)

On one occasion my wife noticed a girl near the back of the audience who responded to all three questions rapidly and enthusiastically. As it turned out, this girl had attended Faith Academy, a MK boarding school in the Philippines. She is typical of the MK which differs from the average American Christian when it comes to dedication.

After the series of questions I would read:

> "And everyone who has left houses or brothers or sisters or father or mother or children or farms for My name's sake, shall receive many times as much, and shall inherit eternal life. (Matt. 19:29)

Dedicating one's children to the Lord is part of the missionary call. Each missionary has to face the possibility of separation from his children in order for them to get a proper education. If parents are convinced that it is God's perfect plan, their children will most likely believe it also.

One of the MK boys we have followed for years has recently graduated from a Christian college and is facing full time Christian work. As a first grader he came to us with tears in his eyes and said, "I guess I don't make a very good boy."

"What is the matter?" we asked.

"Well, I can't get my jeans snapped."

Of course, he was comforted and helped. Boarding schools do present unique challenges but the MK adjusts quickly. A boy just slightly older who was observing all this stepped in to help. He said, "Oh, the way to do it is to hold the snap in place and bump up against the wall. That's what I do."

We have observed that frequently children's problems have been resolved in boarding schools. Sometimes the parents didn't even realize that a problem existed. A rather simple example of this is found in a girl who would not respond to simple greetings. Together the staff was able to convince her of the importance of responding when spoken to.

A more classic example of improvement came about by the staff doing nothing. The child's problem was asthma. Strangely enough the child only had asthma when the mother visited the school. I'm not certain that the mother was ever able to comprehend her part in this.

One mother asked us to see if we could help her son get over the habit of frequently clearing his throat. It was a nervous tic. Every time the boy made the gutteral sound, a member of the staff closest to him would do likewise, then smile at him when he looked up. Soon the children were joining in the fun. Within two weeks the tic disappeared.

The mother of an overweight daughter once asked the houseparents to help her lose weight. They did work on this, only to discover that the mother was sending her cookies and candies. Naturally, a parent who supports and backs up a house parent will benefit.

One of my greatest pleasures is to relate the many success stories among MKs which we have witnessed through the years. But after all, I am biased and there are those who would be glad to relate the way preachers' kids and missionary kids go astray.

Generalization is perhaps the element which clouds the issue. When we meet one bad apple, or one MK gone sour, we may assume that it happens to them all. That's generalization. But for every MK which has turned his back on his parents and God, I am willing to produce the names of at least twenty-five who have not.

Therefore, I was happy to be able to do extensive research in the area of MK personality development. The facts document that MKs in boarding schools, develop personalities very much like those of non-boarders. Out of thirty-two personality traits, MK boarders differed from day students only on one trait. The difference was not great, but the MK boarders are on the average very slightly restrained while the non-boarder is very slightly adventurous. Both boarders and non-boarders develop wholesome and emotionally stable personalities.

So what do boarding schools do to the missionaries' children? They do more than can ever be written. They provide a quality education in a spiritual atmosphere. One might easily get the impression that God works in special ways with the MKs in boarding schools.

RELATIONSHIPS

A newly arrived missionary was surprised when we introduced him
to the missionaries' children as Uncle rather than Mr. So-and-so. He
responded by using the titles of niece and nephew before their names.
The MKs did not catch the joke. Actually, using the titles of Aunt
and Uncle is a long standing tradition in foreign missions. We have not
been able to trace the origin of this custom, but one wonders if it may
not have resulted from the fact that MKs do not generally have blood
relatives on the field; no aunts, uncles, cousins, nor grandparents.

A friend of ours recently included a cartoon in their prayer
letter with the caption, "What do you suppose it will be like when he
learns that grandmother and grandfather are not a cassette recording?"
Parents sometimes seek fellow missionaries to fill the role of relatives.

About three months ago some missionaries whom we admire were
sharing with a small group of us that they had been praying for someone
to be the grandmother and grandfather for their two sons. Later I
asked Louise, my wife, what she thought of it. She expressed what I
was feeling when she answered, "I don't feel like a grandparent." We
weren't ready. I hadn't even reached fifty years yet.

A few weeks later we received a letter from our daughter-in-law.
Louise was reading it aloud to me. About half way down the first page
she read, "More good news. I had my doctor's appointment and the doctor let me hear the baby's heart beat."

Louise exclaimed, "That's an unusual way to announce that she's pregnant." The first letter, it turned out, had been lost in the mail. We would be grandparents, ready or not. Somehow it's hard for many of us missionaries to think of ourselves as grandparents, or aunts, or uncles.

Nevertheless the extended family of each missionary is in the form of fellow missionaries. Families plan to take vacations or go on outings with other families and the relationship equates to that of relatives.

Missionaries seldom have seriously ill, handicapped or emotionally disturbed members. In such cases when these types of situations occur the families return to their home countries. Death of relatives is a rather remote experience for the MK. They may mourn more over a missionary aunt or uncle than they will over even a grandparent. From time to time it has been my responsibility to break the news to an MK that a relative in America has died. The one question I always ask is, "How close were you to him/her?" More often than not, the response will be, "Not too close. I've not been with them very much." Their mourning may be more for the sorrow that one of their parents will be experiencing.

Children tend to relate well to the nationals. They learn the language faster than their parents. They seem to become the leaders. The possession of one toy will do it. On our first assignment to a secluded village we took our children's toys, including a tricycle. The villagers had never seen one of these before. When they asked me what it was I had to look the word up in a dictionary in order to tell them in their own language what it was called. You can imagine what that tricycle did to our children. They were the ones to decide who would and who would not ride it. They became kings of the roost.

People also look up to the white, blond, blue eyed foreigner as unique. A student we worked with showed me how she used to proudly extend her arm so that people could feel it. She knew they wanted to feel her strange skin so she made it easy for them.

This king of the mound superiority which MKs soon feel is one of the reasons that parents often give for wanting their children in MK schools. They feel that it is necessary for the children to be with others, more like themselves, in order to rub off the rough edges.

For the older children there may be a desire to date nationals. Since a discussion of the pros and cons of this subject would be extensive, I would prefer to delay writing on this until a later date. I would, however, like to state that I believe parents may create serious problems by denying a teenager's request to date a national merely on the basis of his/her nationality.

Maids or housegirls are employed by missionaries in certain parts of the world where finances allow for it. A wise missionary will guard against their children becoming bossy and demanding of these household helpers. There have been instances of children so attached to the helpers that they experienced serious depressions upon separation.

MKs may develop poor attitudes toward those in the host country by absorbing statements made by their parents. I've been guilty myself while driving in heavy traffic. I have never sworn in the presence of our children, but they might easily get the impression that I look upon national drivers as stupid and inferior. They may generalize this to include all host country people. Parents' attitudes need modification at times. One faculty member put it this way, "I used to get mad at the people who walked on the road, until I realized they had no other place to walk. Now I look at it as though I am driving on their sidewalk."

Our studies have revealed that MKs choose to have fewer friends, but work at making these intimate relationships. For some time I had suspected that the reason for this might be due to the knowledge that someday there would be a forced separation, and that it would create an emotional hurt.

Then I ran across a statement made by Betty Olsen, an MK who gave her life as a missionary nurse in Viet Nam.

> "I was away from them (parents) eight months out
> of every year. And in high school I was away all year
> with kids whose parents were all over the world. In
> a situation like that, you learn not to make close
> friendships, because as soon as you get attached to
> someone, they leave." (Hefley, 1974, p. 79)

Regarding MK's relationships with their parents there is ample evidence of dedication and loyalty. This is true especially in the case of boarding students. The quality time that boarding students have with their parents is enviable. Vacations are planned carefully since time together is limited. For the parent who has his children at home all the time it is easy to procrastinate, putting off activities such as outings or recreation so vitally important to individual and family morale. The parent may think that there is always next week. For the boarding student, family time is limited. He knows it and his parents know it. So they work together at making the very best of the situation.

In relating to his parents the MK soon learns that there needs to be a delicate balance between the good things and the bad things he says about school. If he says too many good things about the school, the parent will think he doesn't like home. If he gives too many negative comments the parents will wonder about the quality of the school.

One mother confided in me that her son, a grade school boy, had come home bragging about all the fun at school. It was "Uncle Dan this and Uncle Dan that" until she reacted by saying, "Well, after all, Uncle Dan isn't God."

We assured her that when he was at school he bragged about home.

The trends in foreign missions result in a missionary force representing more and more nationalities. The proverbial U.S. and Canadian missionaries are being joined by Australians, New Zealanders, Germans, Japanese and many more. Therefore we are witnessing ever increasing opportunities for the MK to become worldminded. His roommate may be from Holland or Switzerland. Good natured jokes are no longer confined to local origins within the U.S. One joke presently circulating is:

Question: "Do you have a fourth of July in Canada? (Germany, Japan or whatever)."

Response: "No" with an explanation of that country's independence day added.

Question: "Well, if you don't have a fourth of July, what comes after the third?"

Fortunately most MKs learn to love and appreciate the citizens of the host country. They may form close friendships especially with those in the church. They may very likely become actively involved in their parents' ministry by perhaps teaching and playing musical instruments.

One of the big events at Faith Academy each year is the dedication of the school yearbook, The Tiwalan. Over the years dorm parents, teachers, counselors and principals have been honored in this way. Anticipation changes to anxiety as the student body gathers for the presentation assembly. Students quietly exchange their guesses as to who will receive the honor. Faculty members also take a mental inventory as to who might be the person most worthy of the recognition. One year, especially, it seemed that few people could guess who would be honored. However, as soon as the name was given, there seemed to be unanimous approval. The individual was well chosen. She was the friendly, helpful, high school secretary, a Filipina. Where there are missionaries children, there is recognition of quality.

WHAT ARE LITTLE MK BOYS AND GIRLS MADE OF?

Missionary parents might claim that their children (MKs from missionary kids), are made of "sugar and spice and everything nice." Teachers and dorm parents working with MKs would probably agree. But a more accurate description might be found in the results of a recent study of MKs in Faith Academy in Manila, Rift Valley Academy in Kenya, and the Alliance Academy in Quito. The MK personality traits may be defined as: emotionally stable, highly intelligent, reserved, conscientious, controlled, conservative, relaxed, somewhat submissive and slightly group dependent. (Danielson, 1981)

An MK is Emotionally Stable

Results on personality tests indicate that this is the strongest and most predominant personality trait. This suggests a tendency which some have referred to as phlegmatic, and includes emotional maturity, stability and calmness. People with this trait may possess an ability to cope with others without becoming ruffled, to adjust to facts without letting emotional needs obscure the realities of particular situations.

When our family first traveled to the Philippines we were almost embarrassed by the MKs traveling on the plane. They seemed to know all about airplanes and especially the free items available. It did not seem to bother them at all to frequently request food, drinks, games, stationery, books, etc. Nor did they seem to feel rejected when the stewardess had to explain that they were out of a particular item.

99

World travelers occasionally run into an MK in international air-
ports. They are amazed that these children carry their own passports, and
know how to go through the process of ticket counters and customs like
it's "old hat." Frequently these children will be twelve years old or
younger and may be responsible for even younger brothers or sisters.

New missionaries marvel at the way these children handle the situation. They seem calm and confident. When they are engaged in conversation they respond respectfully and are happy to explain that they are
traveling to or from school as well as tell about themselves and their
parents' work. Obviously, emotional stability surfaces very early in the
life of the average MK.

An MK is Highly Intelligent

The second strongest test score average (tying with Reserved described below) is in the area of general intelligence. They tend to grasp
ideas readily and are fast learners with high scholastic mental capacity.
The MK is an achiever.

A sixth grade boy explained a way he uses his intelligence when
he's on furlough. It is similar to stories we have heard from various MKs.
He goes to the store with his grandparents. When they pass by a toy or
item he wants, he stops. The grandparents say, "What are you looking at?"

"Oh, just this toy boat. I've never seen one like this before," he
responds. "We don't have things like this on the mission field."

"Would you like to have one?" they ask.

"It must be very expensive," he responds. "Let's go." But he knows

100

that it is as good as his. Next time he'll use the same tactic with slight variations.

One MK school teacher explained a problem that many teachers in those schools have realized when she stated, "I covered all the material which took a year to cover in the States in less than a semester. These kids are capable of doing good work faster."

The average IQ score of MKs run between 15 and 20 points above the general public in the U.S. The students themselves will tell you that they make better grades in their home countries than on the field. It's not that the teachers are stricter, but rather that they know they can move faster and expect more than they would in the home country.

An MK is Reserved

They may be more penetrating in their evaluation of people and things, more dependable in long term undertakings and in those things requiring exactness, more uncompromising, more earnest and more inventive than the average American child. Some people may see them as critical, skeptical or aloof, but it is this very trait which helps them to keep high personal standards.

The MK does not always know what is the proper way to act in a new situation. But he is keenly aware that different cultures do have specific social procedures. Therefore, he will stand back and quietly observe how things are done before taking part. He may hesitate to ask very simple questions for fear that people will think him dumb. One MK explained that she wanted to know the difference between a malted milk and a milk shake,

101

but was afraid to ask.

Another girl said, "It happens all the time. You just have to go along and pretend like you know. Later when you have a really close friend you can ask them or else your parents. Once in choir I saw some-one using Binaca (a mouth spray) and asked what it was. The girl I asked just laughed at me and told all of the other kids. I could have slapped her, I was so embarrassed."

The reserved tendency of the MK contributes to his general accept-ance in varying situations.

An MK is Conscientious

This factor has a religious aspect. It may be an actual measure-ment of fundamental religious conscience. The tendency is to be exacting, persevering, determined, responsible, emotionally disciplined, organized, conscientious, dominated by a sense of duty, and concerned about morals and rules. It may reflect the extent to which an individual has accepted the values of the adult world.

As a whole missionaries seem to emphasize the attributes of honesty and dependability. While MKs are also susceptible to temptations of cheating, lying and stealing just like all boys and girls, they get very definite, strong and early messages from the parents that those are "No No's."

An MK high school boy once stated that he cheated on a test once when he was in middle school. He copied from a fellow student's paper and got a worse grade than he would have if he had guessed at the answers, according to him. He never did it again. A strong guilt feeling seems to accompany those MKs who cheat regularly.

Many of the MKs are taken aback and uncertain how to react to friends and relatives who brag about ways they use to get messages over long distance phone lines without paying, or being dishonest with income tax returns, or re-using stamps for mailing letters. If values are both taught and learned, missionaries and their children do well.

An MK is Controlled

The MK is probably concerned about his social image and self-concept. He may be precise in measuring up to social standards as he understands them to be. Chosen and effective leaders often possess this trait. It is also associated with success in mechanical, mathematical and productive organizational activities as well as success in school. It is no secret that most MKs returning to the U.S. or Canada, do exceptionally well in school.

The personality trait of controlledness seems to combine nicely with that of reservedness as defined above.

Once there was a scuffle in the hall just outside of my office and a boy was shoved into and broke several of the glass jalousies. This was a startling introduction to a boy whom I came to appreciate more and more as the months went by. He ended up earning an Eagle Scout award.

But the most startling thing about the incident was that we almost never witness knock down, drag out fights in the MK schools, at least on the high school level. The MK feelings can be as strong as anyone's but they are amazingly under control. "Outbursts of anger" (Gal. 5:20) are considered to be deeds of the flesh and not of the Spirit.

An MK is Conservative

This personality factor indicates that a person has, as a whole, accepted what has been taught in the home and at school. It suggests that missionary parents as well as the MK schools have enjoyed a measure of success in imparting to the children a value system much like their own.

It has amazed me through the years that students in MK schools do not seem to cross major doctrinal lines. While they do seem to enjoy some services in other Protestant churches, they remain extremely loyal to their parents' doctrinal position, generally remaining in the same denomination.

An MK once told me he was interested in studying to be a preacher in another denomination. This interest arose because of his identification to an outstanding teacher of that group. We neither discouraged him nor encouraged him. As it turned out he did remain loyal to his parents. There have been instances of missionaries who believe that evangelization consists merely of announcing Christ and His work without emphasizing a personal born again experience. Some of these missionaries' children have had personal experiences of salvation in Christ at the MK schools. Yet they remain loyal to their parents and their denominations.

An MK is Relaxed

The opposite of relaxed (tenseness) is of general concern to the clinical psychologist. Since MKs are relaxed there is little danger of high levels of anxiety over long periods of time. This suggests, as do the other traits, a well adjusted group of individuals. They may be inclined to be sedate, tranquil, satisfied, composed and unfrustrated. This trait makes it easy for the individual to socialize.

In November, 1970, Typhoon Yoling ripped through the Philippines, destroying over 50% of the buildings on the Faith Academy campus. My wife and I had lived through earthquakes and volcanic eruptions but it was our first experience with typhoons.

The boys in the dormitory in which we were dorm parents had for the most part experienced numerous typhoons. In fact, they had prayed for a typhoon so they could have a day off at school. The Lord does answer prayer.

When we told the boys to put all their valuables in the closets and push the bunks up against them, they informed us that nothing would happen, but they did reluctantly obey. In fact, they continued to reluctantly obey when we announced each step of the preparation: close the doors, go to the dining hall, and be ready to go into the half cellar.

They all seemed so certain of themselves, so calm and relaxed. Why couldn't they get excited and tense like us? Fortunately, for my credibility, the typhoon did considerable damage. It was consoling later when they told us we were right after all.

105

An MK is Slightly Submissive

A high school counselor on short assignment to an MK school was shocked to find out that the students "let the teachers give them so much homework." Her counseling style obviously leans toward the assertiveness philosophy. Personally, I find that the majority of counseling problems in the area of authority result from an unwillingness to submit to authority. In fact, when people do submit, they often discover that the authority becomes less demanding.

Problems do arise for adults who are so submissive that they are not able to move out from under tyrannic authority. Notice, however, that MKs are only slightly submissive.

In a world aiming in the direction of assertiveness or aggression, it is exciting from a Christian point of view to find a group of individuals who are willing to recognize and obey authority. Taking into account the conservative value system of MKs we may be assured that there will be submission to God, to parents and to authority in general as long as such authority does not conflict with God's principles. The MK tends to be highly desirable to employers. They can be trusted to do honest and consistent work.

An MK is Slightly Group Dependent

This personality trait of group dependence has to do with a preference to work and make decisions with other people. Individuals with this trait tend to be joiners and sound followers with a concern for the conventional and fashionable.

Several years ago, I was surprised when a graduate of Faith Academy told me that a certain classmate had called him long distance and spent about half an hour on the phone. It wasn't the fact that an MK girl called an MK boy but that they had never been particularly close friends while at school.

Since that time I've known of numerous such calls. The MK feels that he just can't explain himself to anyone as well as he can to another MK.

Reunions of MK schools have enviable attendances both in the U.S. and on the field.

On large campuses, such as Biola College in California, it seems as though MKs all know one another and they plan many activities together. After a year or two they will be deeply involved with other people of like mind.

This seems to be a positive trait from a Christian perspective. The MK understands the need of encouragement and support of fellow believers. True Christian fellowship is not unknown to the children of missionaries. "Behold how pleasant it is for brothers to dwell together in unity." Psalm 133:1.

Of course, it cannot be said that all MKs have all of the above traits. After all, they are humans and individuals. But the odds are that each MK does possess several of the above mentioned traits. The exceptions should not be pointed out as typical.

The study also involved a group of evangelical preachers' children

(PKs) who attend Christian schools in the U.S. The two groups are quite similar. However, scores indicated defensiveness on the part of the PKs. Sixty-seven percent of the MKs and sixty-six percent of the PKs responded that they would consider being missionaries or full time Christian workers.

The question always arises as to the effects of boarding on MKs. The evidence of this and other studies is that there is almost no difference between boarder and non-boarder personalities of the MK. The MK boarder and non-boarder differed only slightly on one factor with the boarder being very slightly restrained while the non-boarder tested to be very slightly venturesome. One wonders if the boarding student, with his varied background, feels less need for adventure.

Sixty-four percent of the MKs responded that they definitely would send their children to boarding schools, whereas only twenty-six percent of the PKs stated that they would. On the other extreme only fifteen percent of the MKs said they would never send their children to boarding· schools while forty-two percent of the PKs responded that they would not.

The importance of this data is to the glory of God who seems to overrule basic philosophies of many psychologists by working in special ways in the lives of the children of missionaries. It's a wonder that more people don't want to be missionaries, just so their children could enjoy the benefits of outstanding personality development.

Are MKs perfect? Perhaps nearly so, but there are a few areas of adjustments for them upon returning to their home country. The same research mentioned above also suggests that they may have certain doubts about their own behavior, their bodies and their abilities. Ask an MK if the people where he grew up stared at him. Frequently the response is "yes." In many instances, the MK has frequently had people touch, rub or pinch him. The nationals often just have to know what American skin and hair feel like. As you can imagine, this might give the impression to the MK that he is physically different. Regarding his behavior, he knows he's not perfect because he knows no one is perfect. His conscientiousness and value system tell him that he should never be satisfied, but should keep striving for better behavior. He might say as did Paul, "not that I have already become perfect, but I press on..." (Phil. 3:12)

As for socializing, the MKs may not feel like they have much in common with the others in the U.S. "If you can talk about the latest TV programs, movies, or popular music, you can get along in the U.S.," one MK recently stated, "and if you're not interested in those three things you may have problems." Another stated that all girls want to talk about in America is marriage and the boys talk mostly about sex. One wonders if this is a defect in the MK or in the U.S. society, so controlled by mass media. The MK might feel that there is little interest on the part of American kids about human suffering and spiritual needs.

Like the MK who expressed her fear of asking what was the difference between a malted milk and a milk shake, assuming that everyone would know and think she was dumb, there is often a holding back on the part of the MK returning to America. However, several studies have indicated that after this initial cultural shock, adjustment is made.

109

While they are undergoing the cultural adjustment to the country of their citizenship, they may seek out others like themselves whose parents were missionaries. MK school reunions in the U.S. are well attended and it is not uncommon for MKs to spend their savings in long distance phone calls to former classmates from the mission field.

In summary, it could be said that the average MK has a well adjusted and integrated personality. The MKs seem to have a world view and philosophy based on moral values similar to those of their parents. Their lives and dedication will no doubt bless those who are privileged to have a personal acquaintance with them.

BACK TO THE COUNTRY OF CITIZENSHIP

On our first furlough, after landing in Los Angeles, we were riding a bus to San Diego when I noticed a field of baled hay. Realizing that our son had never seen bales before I pointed them out and said, "You know what those are?" "Oh, yea!" he said, "they're grass bricks." Pretty good for a pre-schooler. He always has been a brilliant boy.

My father met me at the bus station and when we went to the car I noticed he'd bought a new one, but wondered why he had bought a Chrysler. It was actually a Chevrolet. We were experiencing culture shock. Every furlough it has happened to us. Twice I've returned to the U.S. with suits which were not worn on the field only to find out they were out of style in the U.S.

We try very hard to keep up on the changes taking place in the U.S. but printed news just doesn't do it. On one occasion we expected to see major portions of the larger cities burned to the ground due to the racial riots. We had read it in the local papers.

There is no way to avoid this readjustment to culture. America does not stand still while missionaries spend several years on the field.

In similar fashion, MKs undergo culture shock. Research suggests that the adjustment period will be completed in less than a year. Most MKs will weather the storm well, but a few will fall by the wayside. In most cases those who have worked close to the MKs on the field can predict which will do well and which will not. Those who stumble and fall are usually the ones who struggled with authority on the field. They did not have a

111

good self-image and seemed to harbor some bitterness.

Every now and then a brave extrovert will point the accusing finger
at missionaries and say, "Why didn't you prepare your children for their
return to the U.S. (Canada, or wherever)?" The correct and factual response
is that they have been prepared as well as possible on the field. They
have been prepared almost as well as their parents.

Since it is impossible to prepare them for the innumerable small
details and changes, the preparation must be on a deeper level, on the
level of honesty, friendliness, helpfulness, courtesy, obedience and especially dependence on God.

We can also warn them that they may encounter the necessity to adjust to new responsibilities, different value systems and friendships,
handling finances and indifferent churches. They may have to change their
pace, earn a living, learn to drive, make decisions about vacations, and
learn how to cope with red tape.

Responsibility

Even though the MK knows he will be more on his own, suddenly he
learns that there are areas of responsibility that he never dreamed of.
These newly acquired responsibilities in the case of a college student
are similar to those of all high school graduates.

One MK summed it up when he stated that he suddenly realized that
he would never again be under his parents. He could not put off dental
and medical appointments for vacation times when he'd be home. He'd never
be home again. He could not consult with his parents about job opportuni-

ties nor college courses.

In one case a student was encouraged by a college professor to take calculus even though he had not had the prerequisite of trigonometry. The professor looked at his records and said, "Oh, you've done well in high school and on the college entrance tests. You'll do well."

Naturally, by the time a letter reached his parents it was too late to withdraw. Later he shared his experiences in this way, "I was playing a game with God," he said. "First I prayed asking the Lord that if He wanted me to stay in the course that I'd get a good grade, an A or B. Then I prayed that if He wanted me to stay in the course that I'd get an average grade. Again I changed it to just a passing grade. By the time I realized I was failing it was too late to drop it." This was the boy's first failure, but even in this he learned something of value-- how not to play games with God.

Values and Relationships

MKs get along amazingly well with MKs. They are reasonably certain that others cannot understand their interests. An MK girl observed that if you don't talk about TV programs, the latest rock music or movies, there just isn't much you can talk about because that is all the kids in the States have on their minds.

On one occasion an MK boy could not get into his dormitory room in college because his roommate was entertaining a girl there for the night.

"They don't seem to be interested in the same things as we are," one MK girl summarized. "They aren't interested in commitment, of reaching out and helping others or the people of the world."

Even things that seem small issues to those living in America the MK is likely to wonder about. For example, most MKs would not knowingly allow a clerk to give them too much change. Frequently they will wonder why their teenage counterparts in the U.S. or Canada spend so much money on unimportant things.

All of this may lead to a lack of close friendships and leave the MK with a sense of loneliness. Two MKs who had never boarded on the mission field agreed that they could die on the large college campus where they lived and no one would know it. On the other hand MKs who grew up in boarding schools have a hard time sympathizing with those who suffer from homesickness because they have never been away from their parents.

Finances and Work

A few students at an MK school were happy because they were making $3.00 for a half days work in the student store. This was at a time when the minimum wage in the U.S. was $3.50 an hour. Of course some things cost less overseas. In this case a bottle of pop cost 12¢. Nevertheless, the gap between ability to earn and the cost of things is huge. In fact, in many cases, the MK is not allowed to work because of restrictions on his alien visa.

When the MK does get a job in the home country he may be working alongside of other kids who have been used to earning money. He will have some catching up to do, but will tend to be dependable, staying with one job longer than the average American.

114

An alumnus of Faith Academy returned for a visit and shared his experiences with his first pay check in the U.S.

"When I got all that money, I went out and bought a hamburger and a malt. Then I bought another hamburger. It seemed like it was a lot of money but I just couldn't think of anything I wanted or needed. Of course later I found out that it wouldn't go very far by the time I'd paid the school bill.

The MK may have his first experience at having a checking account. He will probably not have the experience of credit cards for a year or two since his parents do not have credit.

Going into debt is another part of the culture shock, especially for those who take out student loans. But one advantage they will have over many students is that they are used to saving and cutting corners to economize. At a breakfast get-together there w're many left-over pancakes. The cook was going to throw them out, so a girl said, "Don't throw them away, I can use them." Someone spoke up saying, "You can tell she's a missionary's kid." Later she laughed about it when telling her parents. "I never throw food out. We always heat it up for another meal. I guess that really makes me an MK."

Churches

It would be difficult for us to recall all the MKs who have reported to us that they had difficulty fitting into the churches in their home country. Some have used the coldness of church members for an excuse to associate with more worldly crowds. The Christians don't seem interested

in missions, and they seem to ask the wrong questions of the MK, such as
"Do you live in a grass hut over there?" or, "What do you do about sani-
tation?" It is not beyond an MK to respond to such questions by making
it sound like they are true martyrs.

"Yes, our roof is thatched with snakes living in it. Sometimes
they fall on our beds at night and one time a snake fell in the soup on
the table. The floor is dirt and ants come up out of it. The natives
don't eat white people because they consider them sick, but they do eat
one another. Our clothes are fairly good when we first get to the field,
but after four years we are wearing mostly rags." The MKs might have their
fun, but they will usually explain that they were just kidding. Several
MKs were speaking English with a foreign accent on a certain college campus.
Later a student asked what language they had been speaking. After the
inquirer left, the MKs had a good laugh.

We cannot speak for all MK schools, but have conducted surveys in
three of them regarding student attitude toward the church services. The
majority have consistently evaluated the services as one of the best things
about their schools. However, we are aware of some MK schools whose student
bodies seem to feel that anything spiritual or church-related is to be
shunned.

As to why the on-campus church services are rated so highly by students we believe the ingredients are:

1. The dedication of the staff to serve Christ in the best
   possible way in the lives of the children.

2. A desire on the behalf of the staff members to make spiritual truths as attractive as possible.

3. The rotation of preaching responsibilities among parents, staff and special guests.

Therefore the MK who has grown up seeing spiritual victories in the lives of nationals with whom his parents work and has enjoyed regular services at the MK school, services especially designed to meet his needs, may find it difficult to benefit from the home country church meetings.

The best solution for an MK back in the country of his citizenship is to become active in a church which has a strong emphasis on missions.

Change of Pace

The protestant ethic seems to include the idea of working hard so that one can play or relax later. But to the MK there might be a bit of a different philosophy, depending on the part of the world in which his parents work. This other philosophy embraces the idea of playing while you work. "If play interferes with your work, by all means quit your work."

The MK is by no means lazy and is usually the type of worker that employers look for. But he may have a period of adjusting to the rat race, fast pace of the home country. He may have been used to noon breaks in tropical climates. To the MK it may seem that people don't just sit down and talk. They must be doing something all the time. When they do sit down it seems as though it's either to eat or watch TV or both. But since MKs tend to be healthy and robust, they will soon take part in the run around world of their country.

Affluency

Missionaries have made the error of not allowing their children enough funds to purchase the clothes which they desperately need to keep up with their peers. It is not fair to expect them to live out of missionary barrels.

One of our supporting churches takes care of their missionary ladies in a wonderful way. They take the missionary to clothing stores, help them choose clothes which are in style, and pay for them. It is such a good thing that we believe it should be extended to include high school graduates.

The MK will be more cautious with his money. One MK girl who we felt was exceptionally dressed explained to us that she didn't have a lot of clothes, but knew how to combine skirts and blouses with sweaters and scarves into many different outfits.

But the affluency of the American public does cause the MK to stop and wonder. Even the overweight people are hard for the MK to understand, according to one survey.

Vacations

Missionary students may be the only ones in the dormitories when vacation time comes. If they are lucky a friend will invite them to spend the time at their home. Loneliness may be the strongest at vacation times. Other students have a family to return to, but the MK's parents are probably overseas.

Adoptive parents would be very helpful for these periods of time.

Some missionaries have been able to set up small apartments near relatives for their MKs to use when they need them. This is, of course, a
financial drain, but perhaps worth the extra expense. We believe churches and mission organizations both should become active in providing
this minimal amount of security for the MK - a place where the MK may be
assured of room whenever he senses the need.

This may not seem like a big need to the average church goer in the
home country, but we can assure you it does seem important to both the
missionaries and their children.

Driving

The MK returns to his home country, perhaps never having driven a
car, and without a license. The lower age limit for driving in some
countries is eighteen years. So while the American child may have taken
a driver's training course and been driving two years, the MK might be
entering a new experience. He will do well on the written test, most
likely, but if the road test is stringent, he may have to repeat it several times. In general, the MK will be a good insurance risk. The exceptions include a boy who totaled three cars in his first year in the U.S.
Another boy totaled a car on which he had no insurance, thus imposing an
additional financial liability on his parents.

This is another area in which missions and churches could become
active. Why not offer driver's instructions and even good used cars for
the MKs?

Insurance for those MKs who have not had formal training in operating vehicles is excessively high. The difference in insurance fees for those who benefit from recognized training, would in itself pay for a good portion of the expenses.

Red Tape

Filling our forms is difficult for most of us. But what about the MK? On most forms he will get no further than the second line without a question. He can fill in his name without any problem but when it asks for his home address he is apt to say, "Do they mean my address on the field, or the one I'm living at now?" To complicate it further, some forms ask for both temporary and permanent addresses. To most people this seems to be no big problem. But ask any missionary, "Where are you from?" and the response will be revealing. It may start with a laugh and then an explanation of "I'm not really certain." This certainly may be indicative of their identity with Christ who had no where to lay his head.

There has been a considerable amount of red tape involved with foreign residence. MKs have submitted numerous passport and identification photos to government agencies. Their thumb prints have been applied to an endless number of documents. But for the most part this paper work has been handled by mission personnel or parents.

MKs have missed opportunities to receive scholarships thinking that the schools themselves would handle the details.

Even using the telephone might seem to be too complicated. After all, the MK may not have had the use of a telephone on the field. Or if he did he might have been used to waiting long periods of time making the

proper connections only to give up and ride across town to speak to someone.

Someone once observed that missionaries and their children may be
the only ones who wait for the dial tone before dialing. Everyone else
assumes that the phone is ready to use. Our excuse is that we have been
known to spend as long as a half hour waiting for a dial tone on foreign
soil. Few MKs are able to empathize with the American who complains
about "Ma Bell."

How MKs Cope with Adjustment

From a survey of 78 MKs in U.S. colleges (Wright, n.d.) we list
here sixteen methods of adjustment which they used:

1. Prayed

2. Became involved in sports

3. Dropped out of school temporarily

4. Sought to be involved socially

5. Made friends

6. Isolated self, rejected new friends

7. Self-pity

8. Recognized God's will and willing to accept it

9. Confided in the certainty of the situation being God's leading

10. Talked with parents (when on furlough) or wrote to parents on
    the field. Ham radio was helpful to a few.

11. Talked with relatives

12. Struggled with it alone since did not know relatives or others

well enough to confide

13. Rebelled

14. Backslid spiritually attempting to identify and be accepted

15. Worked hard to acquire material possessions

16. Rejected those who were materialistic and found it hard to
    understand the lack of value placed on money by many at school
    and in the churches.

The same study indicated that there is virtually no difference in adjustment between the boarder and non-boarder MK except that the non-boarder
expressed more difficulty in relating to their peers.

Equipped for Stress

Adjusting to stress will face every MK returning to the land of
their citizenship. No one denies it. People do, however, debate whether
or not the MK is prepared to withstand the trials.

It is a strong conviction among many missionaries that MKs are
equipped to handle temptation and this is found in their basic trust in
the Lord.

"No temptation has overtaken you but such as is common to
man; and God is faithful, who will not allow you to be tempted
beyond what you are able, but with the temptation will provide
the way of escape also, that you may be able to endure it."

(I Cor. 10:13)

Some MKs have never acquired such faith. Others who have may not fully
realize the keeping power of the Lord until they begin to experience ad-

justment to their new environment.

Stress in itself can be healthy. "Tribulation worketh patience," etc. (Rom. 5:3) Some metals are improved with stress, or tempering. It is only the extreme that distresses. Weights may be added to an extended wire and when they are removed the wire will return to its original size and shape. That is, it will until too much weight is applied. When removed this will leave the wire permanently stretched or distressed.

Frustration may result in either depression or blessing. The route of depression is fear and self-pity while the path of blessing is acceptance and involvement.

The MK may not feel ready for the stress involved and he may say later that he would have liked to have had a little more orientation, but it's the parents' responsibility to determine if their child actually is ready. If not, there are two possible solutions:

1. Have the child stay on the field to await the next furlough so that he may return to his parents' country with them.

2. Request an early furlough in order to help that child adjust.

In all these matters, there is a perfect solution, and the Lord will not hide it from the faithful, diligent servant.